WALK

TO THE

MOON

The Story of

ALBERT HOUTHUESEN

Albert Houthuesen, photographed by Richard Nathanson in July 1969

'As Well As I Can'

Walk to the Moon is English for the Dutch expression *Loop Naar de Maan* meaning 'Forget it.'

It was how Albert's mother would respond whenever, as a child, he asked her for painting materials.

Cover: *Walk to the Moon, Childhood Admonishment* 1975

Title Page: *Reflections* lithograph

1

5, LOVE WALK,
DENMARK HILL, S.E.5.

June 12th 1968.

My Dear Richard,

Many thoughts go out to you from me upon this your 21st Birthday. Above all I wish you very good health, and a most marvellous fulfillment of the many gifts you have.

You have the hope and spirit to bring these things about, and I believe the coming years will prove these things to be true.

Ever Yours,

Albert.

Albert Houthuesen and Richard Nathanson 1969

Introduction

Albert Houthuesen has told his story in his own words and images. Our conversations, many of them recorded, began in November 1967. They continued, often at weekly intervals, until the summer of 1970; and thereafter more infrequently following Albert's stroke.

We met mainly at weekends, and conversed over tea in the artist's small sitting cum dining room – also in his studio and occasionally in the garden. The photographs taken there convey something of the vitality, range and depth of feeling with which Albert spoke during our conversations.

In 1967, I had seen very few of his pictures. But their beauty and power, and an inner torment I could only sense, moved me indescribably. I was convinced of his greatness and although I knew virtually nothing about him, resolved to make a concentrated study of his work and life.

Our conversations commenced three weeks after we met. I was twenty and my own youthful 'search' did have a natural bearing on the nature and intimacy of our dialogue. Gradually, I began to see that his work, despite its seeming diversity, possessed certain unchanging elements which rendered each image part of a coherent, unified vision. This underlying consistency over sixty years, and sense of completeness – of 'as well as I can' – in even the slightest of his sketches, is understandable given that the work is a direct expression of Albert's own character and experiences; and of his essentially unchanging response to those experiences.

Aside the two lithographic images of 1926, the lithographs reproduced were made during the last ten years of his life. For me, they vividly touch upon and heighten a particular moment described or idea expressed. And show, as do his words, how intensely he was able to relive and evoke the past, even from early childhood. No image is more tragically present than 'Stone Cutter' (Page 18). For Albert, the clown is a symbol, inseparable in spirit from the artist and the poet. Many portray the clown as philosopher and saint.

Albert introduced a still very young man eager to see the world, to the notion of 'an inner journey'. That an enquiring, 'seeing' imaginative mind could, without travelling the globe, gain an understanding of the underlying, universal elements that link all living things and Nature, regardless of time or place.

'Walk to the Moon' describes an inner journey. A moving backward and forward in time. And indeed beyond time, with all three states fusing into a single, creative entity. Any true insight into Albert's creative process precludes his images and the events of his life from being presented in a strictly chronological order – as evidenced by his realising certain themes and individual pictures over many years. Albert once said 'We walk in mystery.' And if this book gives some sense of a spiritual, creative state of being, it will have attained its objective.

It is also my hope, these many years later, that Albert's compassion, wisdom and humour; and his wonderfully expressed veneration for the beauty and mystery that surround and greet us at every turn, will joyously inspire those of a younger generation discovering their own way.

Richard Nathanson

Contents

Amsterdam

It is one of the great ironies in my life to recall with you the early days. To think that now my workroom is full of white canvasses yearning. In the profoundest sense they still defy me, but now they are there to be used.

Mama's father died at the age of twenty-eight when she was three years old. He had been a musician and an actor in London. I imagine her mother's second marriage upset her. Having to accept a stepfather and eventually stepbrothers and sisters. That is when the battle began and there were certain things Mama could never grasp. Her mother met her second husband, a Houthuesen and an uncle of my father, in Holland. And they came to live in London.

Mother's first communion c.1883

Mama was educated in a convent. This photograph taken of her at first communion is of a good, innocent child. And when I look at it and think of Mama's upbringing in this convent, it's incredible that this girl becomes a woman who is never wrong in anything, with whom there is never any question of discussion. And from whom my sister and I and my two brothers, as children, never heard a word of endearment.

When Mama was eighteen, she returned to Holland to look after her grandparents. Her grandfather, Nicholas Weidemeyer, retired there after being, for many years, conductor at the Crystal Palace, playing chiefly Handel. There has always been this musical and theatrical background on both sides of my family which intrigues me very much.

My father Jean-Charles Pierre Houthuesen was born in Amsterdam in 1877. His father, Johannes, had married Charlotte Houlier. One day, my father and Johan Buziau, his first cousin who became a famous clown, called at my great-grandfather's house where Mama was staying. They were both mad about her. The door was open and Mama heard Papa say 'Ja, dat is her.'* And she saw the lined face of the clown, and a good-looking, charming young man who, when they came in, sat down and played the piano.

She fell in love with him. And from that moment, it was poor Papa; and Johan was spared.

Father at Eighteen*

My father worked at his Uncle Houllier's piano factory, but his real desire was to become a painter. At the wedding breakfast, he suddenly announced his decision to leave the family piano business and devote himself to painting. Everyone was very shocked because they had hoped he would continue with his music.

*Albert thought his father's melancholy expression was because he felt his love of painting to be completely misunderstood by his family. Albert remembered the Dutch for 'Yes, that is …' but not for 'her' – 'ze'.

Wedding 1901

After the marriage, Papa painted himself and Mama
in their wedding clothes – a life-size portrait.
Can you imagine how much in love he was with her?
And within a few years, the poor man was so unhappy
that he himself destroyed the canvas.

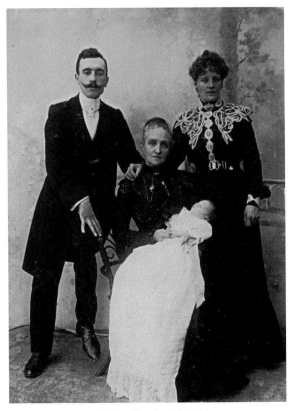

Albert at three weeks held by Grandma McFedries

Albert commented on his father's right hand; and the 'Frenchness' of his face. Also on how apart his mother and father already seemed, adding 'The first-born usually brings happiness to the parents.'

Albert 1904*

Late summer and autumn are the happiest seasons for me, perhaps because I was born in October. I think all these things are very important. When one happens to be born. And at what time and where. There's only one place to be born and that is in Amsterdam.

I remember the Albert Cuyp Straat as something very boring with commonplace architecture. I am amazed at how much I do remember. For instance my first walk to the Rijksmuseum and not knowing what it was, peering through huge windows and seeing the ancient flags of Amsterdam. Then going into museums and finding out how the Dutch were victors everywhere. I do vaguely remember seeing marvellous things – for instance a lamp-lit scene by Gerard Dou.

Small Clown Vignette lithograph

*Albert's mother was proud of his 'pumped up' appearance. Albert thought he looked far too fat, but approved the hat.

J-C.P Houthuesen 263 Albert Cuypstraat (Albert's first home) 1903   AHT

As a child I made visits to Zandvoort, and the sea just put the wind up me. My memories are not at all of this summer holiday effect that most children are supposed to have, paddling in the sea. I was terrified of its power. Once, walking along a dyke and looking onto rooftops on the other side, I can remember being very frightened about the idea of the sea level – seeing and thinking what it meant and feeling that in some ways it was a complete illusion.

I was much happier in Amsterdam, walking on streets which I felt couldn't be inundated, as if they couldn't. I think this feeling was instilled in me by Mama. If one crossed from the bank onto a friend's boat then, to Mama, the plank was

Albert 1909

always far too narrow and dangerous. I remember walking with her along the canal. We'd just crossed the Amstel Bridge and to her consternation and my horror, there was a drowned peasant in a great blue fisherman's overall. And Mama, instead of making little of it before a small child, made a tremendous drama.

Albert, by his father 1907   AHT

One vivid memory of school was the playground at the back which was a considerable sandy area simply going into a flat landscape of fields. I remember digging with other boys into the sand and this being my first lesson in what Holland was literally built on. Digging down about four or five feet, making a largish hole in which we played with spades, getting to mud and then to water. That put the wind up me. But I enjoyed school. I loved it. We made family visits, as families do. Sometimes I was very bored, driven to distraction having to eat things one didn't want. And like all children, feeling ghastly at being petted and told to smile. I remember being taken by Mama to a family of actors and actresses and being grumbled at like mad when we left because, for some reason, I hadn't smiled, whereas I had in fact been absorbed with interest.

One day, we were invited onto a yacht on the Amstel, owned by a man called Siebelhoff who was the husband of my father's aunt. I remember him absolutely enchanting me. He was sitting in an armchair and I was standing beside him. He got out a pad of paper and drew on it four lines. Then he asked me what these four lines were. To me, they were just four parallel lines. And I said something like 'four lines that all look the same'. Gradually he added something and something else, and then suddenly the whole thing became a four-masted schooner. I thought this amazing and I shall never forget what it did for me – these few lines being transformed into this fully-rigged four-master schooner sailing on the sea.

Albert c.1910

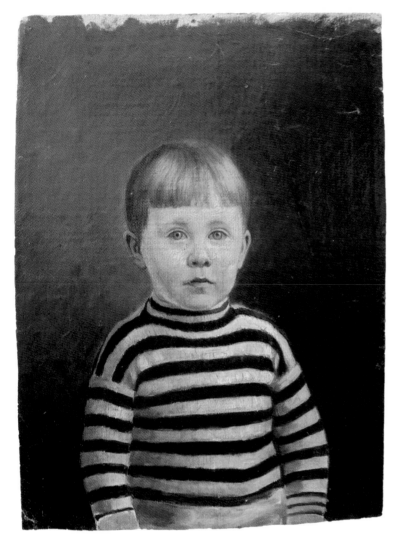

Albert, by his father 1909

I have always deeply regretted not being able to play the piano as my father could really play it. Papa adored the Dutch street organs and where it was then usual to throw a farthing from the window, he would throw sixpence. Of course we children used to dance to it or rush out onto the balcony where, upon one amazing occasion, John in his excitement stuck his head through the railing of this little balcony and began to scream. I couldn't get his head out until I got a foot against the railings and gave a tremendous tug.

Albert, by his father on 26th November 1910
(Note the intensity of the eyes in both drawings)

My feeling for my father by me grew and grew. It became stronger and stronger. And I think it would have done so naturally since he encouraged me. I remember going again and again into the attic in which he worked and being absolutely fascinated being there whilst he painted away. That was the world where I wanted to be.

I remember wanting to be grown up and able to sit on the same sized chair and use the same sized table and palette. It was agony for me to have to climb onto the table to see the palette and what was on it. And my knees ached because I had to kneel on a chair to draw at the table. One drew all the time.

Certainly when I was eight, although like many another youngster I had started to paint and draw before then, I knew I wanted to become a painter.

J-C.P. Houthuesen Japanese Dolls c.1909   AHT

Charlotte c.1910

14

J-C.P Houthuesen Clown with Bell 1911

J-C.P. Houthuesen Apples in a Basket 1909

J-C.P. Houthuesen Japanese Women with Lighted Lantern 1911

My first drawings were all burnt; but I have a fragment of the drawing I was making when this frightful thing happened to my father. It is a burnt fragment of a horse. To me, it seems very symbolic because that horse drawing was the one which my father, before this awful row, had praised in these last words, 'He does it better than I do.' It is simply frightful to think that this encouragement was the sudden beginning of the sudden end.

I walked out of his room. There was a terrible feeling of tension. This situation where my mother felt that one more painter in the house was too much to bear because of the struggle which, by then, they were having. It was simply because I was the eldest that I saw what happened. The things I know and saw going on. I'm the only one who does remember. Charles was a baby of literally six weeks old. Mama had him in her arms. I remember her. Can you think of this terrible thing happening with a six week baby in her arms?

On my way out I heard agonized cries. I hurried back and saw my father stagger into the bedroom, clutching his head between his hands, roaring 'My head, my head'. My demented mother followed him, her shoe in her hand. As he lay on the bed he handed her his purse...........then my father beckoned to me to go to him and I couldn't move and I couldn't speak. Mama was standing at my left, rocking herself to and fro, absolutely demented and beside herself – the only time I've seen this is when I've looked at the telly and seen some primitive remote islander in a trance.

16

Think of this poor man who wanted to embrace me and he didn't even get that. Then he told me that I must look after my Mama and my brothers and my sister. I couldn't answer him. In my mind I said 'Yes I will.' But I couldn't even answer.

I can't quite remember how one left that scene. I think Mama pushed me out of the room with herself too and then sat down in a chair, still rocking backwards and forwards like a madwoman. By then, I imagine, neighbours must have called. An uncle came in and after that I, Charlotte, John and the baby were taken away. But all that becomes very confused.

One of the most vivid memories, after my father died, was of a man calling at the flat. Mama was by now subdued, although still frequently in a state. It turned out that the man was calling for father's army uniform; and the bundle was given to him. He said 'Madame, I am so terribly sorry this has happened,' and Mama was saying 'Ja, ja, ja, that's life' and so on. The man again commiserated and Mama half-wept. I walked over to the window because I couldn't bear it. And they were now saying 'Well fortunately, he is so young, he won't remember a thing about it. None of them will.' Can you imagine what I thought? I have many other memories, as any child does. But that's one of the most oddly vivid. This idea that children forget. They don't.

I can only think that the people who attended my father must have known the truth. But they were kind and thought this situation so ghastly that if it became a court case it would be manslaughter.

I can't talk about it in medical terms, but women having had a baby are sometimes mentally disturbed. And this terrible frustration of Mama wanting more money; and Papa painting that sort of imaginative thing. And the hopelessness of it all.

But in fact Mama hadn't such a bad life. When I think of the people who called on us at the flat, and the laughter that I heard. The artists who came and the singers and pianists. They were an amazing crowd, very reasonable and very gifted people, as one knew later on. And after all, Mama had four well-formed and healthy children. It was just this disaster of Father's desire to be a painter. In ten years after his marriage, he was dead. And in ten years all the work had been done.

This terrible thing that I had witnessed. And afterwards Mama saying that this incident was my fault because Papa had jumped up into the air whilst playing with me and pierced his head on the chandelier base. From that time on, everything was my fault. The very fact that one wanted to draw and paint meant that instead of being the mainstay on whom poor Mama depended, I was only a liability.

Stone Cutter lithograph

All my life I have heard those terrifying cries of my father. Scarcely a day has passed when this terrible scene has not been re-enacted. It has haunted me all my life.

1912 Six months after father's death

London

With proceeds from the sale of Jean-Charles Houthuesen's work, Albert's mother opens a boarding house. This fails. And the family move to London to live with Albert's maternal grandmother McFedries and the mother's three half-brothers at 7 Constantine Road. Tension between mother and daughter makes the situation impossible. And Albert's mother opens a boarding house at 20 Constantine Road.

Clown Fisherman lithograph

The break of coming over to London was very tough, but for a child of eight, who suddenly begins living in a strange and foreign town where he can't even speak the language, everything was also fascinating. I remember the excitement of beginning to travel by train. But what thrilled me was the English landscape. I'd never seen anything so beautiful. At that moment, I didn't care two pence about leaving that pancake land. As we travelled in the train, looking down and up at the embankments covered with flowers and clumps of trees, suddenly there would be, to me, an enormous hill.
A huge rolling landscape. I'd never seen anything so beautiful in my life.

Traffic Signals lithograph

London was a staggeringly beautiful place. I remember first going onto Hampstead Heath and into Hyde Park. And to me they were huge. The trees were enormous. It wasn't at all like the formal park in Amsterdam. It was all on a much bigger scale, and everything moved at a much faster pace. When one wanted to buy things in the shops here, nobody had time for conversation. When a number twenty-four double-decker bus draws up and on you clamber, it's a tremendous excitement for a child who's only clambered onto single-decker little trams. Charlotte and I thought everything was much more exciting. Much bigger. Much noisier.

Constantine Road where we lived, was completely flat. There at the end, was Pond Street which, to me, simply went up like a ladder on end. Quite mad. And then a little way along it went down. I've always said that when we came to London, it was sheer luck that we lived, as it were, on Hampstead Heath. The miracle of England is this marvellous and variable landscape which has everything.

Everything was astoundingly different. My memory was like a slate which had been marked and was being rubbed out. Having this always-to-be-suppressed memory, it's just as well that one was completely absorbed.

John, Charlotte and Charles c.1913

This photograph is so pathetic to me. I couldn't bear to join the group because, quite apart from my own situation, I felt so desperately sorry for my sister and two brothers. If my father could have seen the children he knew like that – Charlotte with parts of her hair cut off because we were lousy: and this boy, my brother Charles, whose hair Mama grew right down to his shoulders.

The whole thing was over with an absolute guillotine when I was barely eight. This tragic running away from Amsterdam was really a flight. And through this particular madness of Mama's, we were not even allowed to speak Dutch in the house. It puzzled me for years. And it has harmed and damaged one's life terribly.

Look Out Ruisdael 1912 watercolour, pencil   AHT

This is only a child's drawing and I don't think, in one way, that it should be taken too seriously. But it's quite obvious that I had seen something I thought looked like this woman with washing on the water and cows standing in the water and that very flat horizon with poplar trees and pollarded willows. Certainly I remember very vividly on one or two occasions – and of course I had no skill to do anything about it – approaching these windmills closely and being amazed at their size. To me, they were gigantic, staggering things.

It's a Dutch landscape from memory. A rival to Hobbema and Ruysdael. Look out Ruysdael! No, any child going away, leaving its country, would make some sketches from memory like that.

When Mama brought us to London, we first stayed with her mother whom I remember as a very charming woman. Once there was a scene between them and suddenly I heard Grandma McFedries accuse mother of killing father. That was frightful for me, but the extraordinary thing is that Charlotte and certainly the boys don't remember or know anything about it.

The other thing was that all religion had gone. In Holland we were brought up as Catholics. Now if Mama, on coming to London, could have gone to the Priory Church in Hampstead and taken any sort of help that the priests offered, it might well have made things much better for her. Sometimes she would get into the most terrible states at home and fly out of the house. I would think 'My God, what is going to happen now?' I would follow her – she didn't know this of course – to the Priory Church. And the moment I saw her enter I knew she would come home.

Mama was always wishing she were back in Holland. And I would ask her why we didn't return. She said 'Yes, yes' and finally 'We will'. For weeks the planned trip was kept a secret between us. The bags were packed in secret on a Friday night. And the next morning we set off, Mama carrying Charles and a suitcase. I a case. And Charlotte and John a brown paper bag each. We marched round the corner to the bus stop; and a Bobby, obviously sympathetic to this quite pathetic-looking troop, asked if he could help in any way. Mama said she was going to

John, Charlotte, Charles and boarder

Liverpool Street Station and from there to Holland. 'To Holland?' he said, 'and have you tickets and all the necessary papers?' 'No', she said, 'I can get them there.' He advised her to go home again. And after some humming and hawing we did. I was shattered.

Curtain Raiser lithograph

Clown and Wife lithograph

Fleet Road School

Albert, John and Charlotte c.1913

My mother quarrelled violently with every one of our relatives. That is why eventually I had to go to my school for London County Council boots, because by then Mama was on her own. And you can understand why that was. She had this terrible thing to hide which was literally kept a secret to her dying day.

Albert (fourth up on the left-hand aisle) c.1913

When I arrived in London I couldn't speak a word of English. At school the first thing that happened was that the clothes were foreign. In winter I had a cap and a fur-lined jacket which the other boys didn't have; and I felt odd in these odd clothes. Sometimes it was a bit rough going. There were the usual school bullies but there were lots of marvellous boys and marvellous games.

I used to adore leap frog. And there was one absolutely wonderful game which I've never forgotten. At one end of the playground was a long wall with two right-angled walls, about eight feet, then twenty feet, then eight feet. And the boys would cluster in each corner. These two groups, each of about thirty boys, had naturally a leader – always that happens doesn't it? One group was 'The Romans' and the other group 'The Ancient Britons'. I was asked – this is terribly funny – to join 'The Ancient Britons'; and with these cheer-leaders, I learnt amongst my first few words of English. When this particular game was over – the whistle having blown – the whole thing had to stop just like that. 'We are the Britons' were literally amongst the first words that I learnt. And the others were shouting 'We are the Romans'.

Whether it still survives I don't know. But these two groups used to work each other into such a frenzy that simultaneously they would shout 'Charge' and there would be a most tremendous crash of heads and arms and bodies and legs; and then the extrication and running to the other end. I was often wounded. There was always of course the eternal quarrel until the whistle blew. Oh, they were marvellous boys. There was one boy called something Churchill. It would be about twenty years ago now, just after the war, when I was walking down Edgware Road; and a man was standing in the gutter crying 'Daffodils'. I bought a couple of bunches, and as we made this exchange, I said 'Good heavens, Churchill'. And he said 'Good heavens, Houthuesen'. I said 'How are you?' 'You can see how I am, can't you?' he said. It was absolutely tragic with this particular boy. He said 'I don't want you to buy any more you know.' I had bought some more, I was so overcome. I said 'No, I want more.' That was the last I saw of him – my school friend Churchill.

Albert at the back (next to the little girl in front of the teacher by the door) c.1913

I remember that maypole. I loved it when we did this sort of hop, skip and a jump march. Sometimes I would furtively look up at this pole to see what a beautiful pattern all these ribbons were making.

25

Clown in Chalk lithograph

At school, since I couldn't speak English, I had to quickly learn all the names of things. The mistress one day gave me a box of chalks and pointed to a blackboard of about four feet by five. Then she pointed to the coloured chalks and asked if I would like to draw. She got a box. I stood on the box and drew an enormous singing thrush with a marvellously speckled breast, perched on an inadequate twig and entirely taking up from one end of the board to the other. Then a wonderful thing happened because it proved to me at once, for the first time in my life, that art knew no barriers. And it was very funny.

The mistress was amazed at this drawing. She promptly called it 'The Castle Thrush' and asked in the teacher from the next class. He walked in, smiled, nodded and patted me on the head. I didn't know what was happening. Then someone else came in, which to the great joy of all the pupils, held up the lesson. Then the headmaster came in and, being a powerful man, he said, 'Very good'. If only some genius could then have said, 'From now on this boy should say to hell with his arithmetic and geography and woodwork'– spending a morning trying to fit the blade into a plane which, when it fell out, was a danger to everybody.

Anyway this drawing was up for a couple of days. Then an amazing thing happened which absolutely took the wind out of my sails. One morning, the mistress pointed to another boy who had been given a job to do by this same charming teacher. He had something in his hand which I couldn't see and he climbed onto the same box I had climbed. From one top corner of this board he went like that, and I could see at once that it was damp because where the sponge had gone it was intensely black. And he went that way and this with a tremendous look of triumph. My poor thrush was gone forever. And I was very upset. I had some idea that this fragile thing would last forever. That was my first mystery. I was so upset that when the board was dry, the teacher came over and, giving me a box of chalks, urged me to draw. But I couldn't do it again.

At other lessons, I scribbled away like the others. Arithmetic with a sadistic master who ruled through the cane was sheer hell. But when drawing lessons came round I always cheered up. Later on I graduated to the art class under a Mr Jones and that was my happiest time. He was a gentle and charming man.

20 Constantine Road c.1913

Of course the Houthuesen children all needed advice in relation to their studies. When reasonable people want their children to get on and, if they have no money, to get scholarships, they go to the priest or schoolmistress, if they have no-one to advise them, and get some advice. But Mama was absolutely on her own. She went her own way and asked nothing from anyone. Or she insulted them. We were exiles and should have been thankful to be over here; but Mama gave the impression that this family with a very foreign name could do nothing but grumble, which was the last straw and asking for it. She had tremendous tenacity, there's no doubt about that. And it nearly killed us all. Everyone was wrong. She was right. And she had to be right over everything. Everything was marvellous at the school in Amsterdam and everything was absolutely ghastly in Fleet Road School. So I don't think the Houthuesen name was looked upon with pleasure.

Mama would have been marvellous as a courtesan or an actress. She had tremendous powers of making herself believe that what she imagined was absolute fact. One day Mama was complaining about Constantine Road. And I suggested we go and stand on Parliament Hill. We could see the Tower Bridge and I said to Mama, 'There's London and if we can't get a living in this great town, there must be something wrong somewhere.' There was St Paul's and Tower Bridge. And between these two points, was the Batavier Line. It was curious to think that if we had money we could simply get on the Batavier Line and go back to Amsterdam. Mama said 'Yes' and began literally to see boats on the water. She had this fantastic imagination.

Mother and Charles 1913

27

My memories of the First World War are of tremendous bangs and people running in the streets, going into the Belsize Park tube station and sheltering with hundreds of other men, women and children. One night there was a raid and the guns on Parliament Hill had blazed away at the zeppelins. The next morning, boys from the school descended upon the tramline in Constantine Road and in Agincourt Road and very nearly had the tramlines up for shrapnel. In fact the police had to control these passionate souvenir hunters. But a curious thing was that I didn't take my piece of shrapnel like every other child because I realised that if I did, the tramline would be up. That doesn't mean I didn't want a piece of shrapnel – I probably did – but something made me stop.

For some the bread queue was a tragedy. It shamed and upset me terribly, but there were many children whose homes had been much rougher from the very beginning; and they weren't upset or ashamed. The other thing was the eternal visits to the pawn shop. It happened every week, every fortnight, every month. And it was far more horrid than standing in the bread queue.

Rembrandt

How I found it I don't know, but in the Finchley Road there was a library and I joined. I remember having to answer all sorts of questions. I couldn't find the books on art in this, to me, huge place, so I went to the secretary at the counter. She took me to a shelf where it said 'Art, Painting, Ceramics'. And to my amazement, I found a large, heavy and marvellous volume on Rembrandt. I couldn't believe that I might take this book home. It became my companion for weeks. And at the end of each month, I would have to bring it back and have it renewed. It was a good inch thick and I remember thinking 'What an incredible life it must have been for anyone to write an inch thick book about it'. But I don't remember the author or the publisher. In one sense that and all the literature in it didn't mean very much to me because, like a sensible book, a scholar's book, it started off sketching the time in which the man lived. The only thing that mattered to me was how he painted these marvellous portraits and made these wonderful drawings. I couldn't really grasp or understand how etchings were made or how paintings were made except that I knew that for painting you had to have wet paint and then it dried and so on.

But I took this thing home – it was filled with reproductions – and I remember saying to Mama, 'Look at this wonderful book that I've been allowed to borrow'. And Mama said 'Well now, yes, yes, you look after that you know'. And then I put a light brown paper cover on it, because everybody at home would take tea, and there would be the book and there would be somebody drinking a cup of tea; and the cup of tea would be put on the book.

My real picture-looking adventures started at the National Gallery and that shook me. I was absolutely amazed and delighted to discover the landscapes by Albert Cuyp because I was born in the Albert Cuyp Straat and his was one of the first names I had learned. That these landscapes were worth hanging well in these huge galleries was proof to me of what a really great nation the English were. I think, by the way, that Turner had his head screwed on when he looked at Albert Cuyp and thought 'My goodness'. 'The Large Doort' in the National Gallery is a most beautiful Chinese-like picture. A noble picture.

My first memory of Rembrandt is of the old self-portrait; and then the earlier one –
beautifully drawn. And of course, with that went all the other masters. Teerboch, Jan Steen,
Vermeer, the Jan Van Eyck panel and his two portraits. Artists like that, they're supreme.

I would wander through the Gallery and then a picture would hold me absolutely;
or I would go and see a particular thing like a Memling or wonderful Italian paintings,
early or late. And I loved an artist like Joachim Patiner and his mysterious rocks. I
remember being pretty disconcerted by the Vincent and not really understanding it.
But being attracted by this mysterious, bright and very roughly painted picture. I didn't
understand what is, for me, the incredible approach of Vincent. To me then, it was rough
whereas Rembrandt was absolutely amazing.

Well, I have never got to the bottom of these miracle things. Often it would become late
and I would have to go. And hurrying out was hell. I can't tell you what I have got out of
the National Gallery. The sheer joy that place has given me. It has made up for all my
non-travelling.

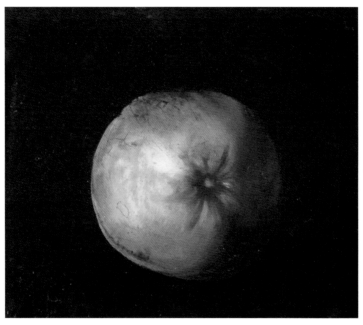

Apple 1917   AHT

The first paintings I made were on cigar-box lids; and the theme, I suppose, was one of
loneliness. They were of monks brooding over skulls and crucifixes in dimly-lit cells –
romantic childish notions of men who thought. There were several of them and like
many other things, they simply disappeared.

I was baptised in a Catholic church and I think that this early training and the early
Christian ideas helped inspire these pictures. I attended the Priory Church in Hampstead;
and for a brief moment I joined the choir and imagined that I was an angel. I did not sing
like an angel and I was often very late. Mama quite literally believed that if I didn't go
to the church to absolve the sins of all of us, we should be damned into hell.

I was given the oil paints by the art master at Fleet Road School. The cigar-boxes were my father's. And I broke up these mementos of Papa because I had nothing else to paint on. The first survival is this one apple on a black background. I remember thinking, as I painted it, that if the light was like that and there was another apple behind and another behind that, then the particular intensity of that light would gradually diminish and diminish. And to me, at that time, this was a very exciting discovery. To me now, this little painting is the product of a time that had to be secret and to oneself.

Nobody in the house made any comment. And if I took the apple up to the room where I painted it, it only meant that at that moment a boarder was away; and this tiny room was vacated and I worked on it by candlelight at night. Had I been in happier circumstances, I don't think this painting would have been as introverted and secret a thing as it is.

Onion and Potatoes 1917   AHT

Just as the next one of a couple of potatoes and an onion is also rather a dark secret painting. And in the third picture of a lighted candlestick, I see something secret too. It's as well they were, because other things that were public in the house were so mauled by idiotic criticism that I myself destroyed many of them. Afterwards, I painted some larger still-lives and other scenes; and a very romantic self-portrait which were all destroyed.

I was absolutely two people. Once I started painting in that little room I led my own true life. All the other was an exasperation. Mama's constant refrain was 'Why doesn't he work for his living' – her attitude all her life. And she lived to be ninety-two.

St Martin's School of Art

When I was fourteen I left school. And by the way I couldn't wait to leave. Whilst still at school, I was already working as a grocer's errand boy. And my first job was as assistant to a grocer in Belsize Park.

Pay-in book November 1917

I served behind the counter, doing it with a solemn face and wondering about the lives of all the beautiful women customers.

The boarders who came and went were from every sort of home. And among them were some very colourful characters. In the early days, I simply got down to working in the house with everybody else. Boots and knives had to be cleaned, tables laid, the cauldron for the baths stoked; and the pails of hot water for the boarders carried up. The landlord refused to do anything about the hot water system which did not function saying 'Do you want the rent to go up?'

There must sometimes have been eight or ten staying in the house with their rooms used as double rooms. The variety of it was amazing, and the tales I could tell. But it was more remarkable for an author than for someone with a longing to paint. It was frightful when the house was full, which it had to be if it was going to pay. At the top of the house were two rooms. One was very small; and if it was empty I could sleep there. The other was small and the whole family slept in that one room. For years it went on and sometimes Mama slept in her armchair downstairs. When a boarder left and a room was empty, Mama would say 'I don't know what will happen' which meant that as the eldest, I could sleep in that room.

Lighted Candle 1917   AHT

I had, by chance, noticed a board outside the Fleet Road School with an advertisement for evening classes at St Martin's School of Art. I went along and was told to bring some drawings and, to my intense joy, I was enrolled. I went every night from seven-thirty to nine thirty. And that was my first experience of meeting other youngsters, many very amusing and bright youngsters whom I felt were years in advance of me. Some were as old as twenty and had already had vast experience.

St Martin's was very charming and rather old fashioned, with a convent next door. The classes were very simple and informal. And at the end of the day it was paradise for me. Sometimes at work I used to be sick with anxiety in case I might have to stay behind for an hour or so, as did occasionally happen, which I knew would ruin my evening.

I was already at St Martin's when I painted this candle. It was very exciting for me to watch what happened to that piece of curtain which I had pinned against the wall when I lit the candle. For me it was a discovery. It's an empty box and the last match has spluttered out. I remember thinking 'It is like life.'

I imagine that this and many another picture of mine is influenced, to this day possibly, by what I saw of my father's work. Papa had this imaginative side. He was fascinated by lanterns lit at night. This room – the isolation of it with the candle and the colour – is perhaps something of the same. One doesn't think about these things at the time. But they are there all the time, until the end of one's life.

I showed the candle painting at St Martin's Sketch Club. The artist who gave the critique on that occasion being a painter called Harold Speed. This was painted very thickly on the canvas; and the class roared with laughter when he said that it was quite obvious that this painter had intended to make the candle-grease real by making it thick. It confounded me at the time because one does certain things quite seriously; and then suddenly to hear a roar of laughter is upsetting. That is a vivid memory, that roar of laughter.

Inscribed by Albert on the back of the Candle painting:

The two holes in the canvas were caused by Mother putting her scissors through it – the malicious jabs of a madwoman. I happened to come in at that moment and she stopped immediately. I said nothing but felt profoundly unhappy.

These three still-lives simply happen to be survivals. And the wonder is that they have survived.

Bust of a Young Woman* 1920 pencil

One had first to enter the 'antique' class. I think it should have been the other way round with the 'life' class first. I shall never forget my first experience of seeing casts of early Greek, Syrian and Italian things. To me, they were an absolute revelation. Many of these drawings were lost. But I have this one drawing of a Florentine bust which enthralled me. It was so beautiful and I remember drawing it during the long, light summer evenings.

*Drawn from a plaster cast of the Desiderio da Settignano marble in the Bargello Museum, Florence.

I can't tell you the names of the original artists but there were some noble things. I can remember spending hours looking at a cast of the eye of Michelangelo's *David*, imagining the size of the whole carving. Afterwards, I was allowed to go into the 'life' class; and I found trying to draw from the figure a most amazing and miraculous thing to do.

Clown with Double Ruff lithograph

The agony was one so wanted to get on with one's drawing and painting. And the only thing that in fact stared one in the face was that Monday morning meant a particular job that one had to go to. I saw literally no future at all in relation to how I was going to draw and paint, to the extent that I wanted to draw and paint. I remember one Sunday evening I was with a friend and just about to go home. I thanked him and then I groaned 'Oh, Monday morning, confound Monday morning!' And Nicholas's mother said 'Well, you know we all have to do something to live' which was, of course, absolutely true. Only too true.

I left the grocer's and was out of work. How I found the Periscope Prism Company I don't know. It was a factory in Hampstead where, during the '1914-18' War, they ground lenses and made periscopes for rifle sights; so that you could murder your enemy so many more yards away with so much greater accuracy.

I was given a piece of metal to copy. I had to cut this into a certain shape with files. And in relation to how I did this job, I would get the job at the factory.

Well, I made what I could of it. I took it back and the foreman there said 'Yes, alright, you've got the job.' And that was that. I next had to cut things with hacksaws, and then, enduring the most ghastly and obnoxious smells, I had to boil these periscope metal block tubes. I was always thankful when this was over – it was a lower grade job. Then they were handed over to an older boy who fitted, I think, four lenses into this thing. There was a hair-breadth wire section across the lens which made it an accurate telescopic sight. Then you screwed on these ends with the lenses in them which were also marked. The boy who got the job to put in these lenses then delivered them to the office where the foreman examined them.

There was a terrible row and he was instantly sacked, poor fellow. He was out because he'd not only left a great deal of dirt on the lenses, but he'd cracked most of them with over-screwing. I was given one of these wretched things to start again. I was such a priggishly clever coward you know, it's ghastly. I was told to clean one of these little lenses and fit the wires. And of course, Albert did it perfectly. There were no cracks, no lenses were broken. Oh God! They were so perfectly done that I got the job and other boys came along and had to do the boiling of the tubes.

Laurel lithograph

The one remarkable thing that happened there was that I worked in what was called 'The shop' at the end of which was an office where the girls worked. It was discovered that I was a precocious lad; and one day, one of the girls asked 'Do you love me?' or something like that. So I wrote her a note. There was a space in the glass partition, so I put this note, this passionate letter, through this slot in the wood to her. One girl was absolutely shocked that a boy so young should know so much. The others roared with laughter that one so young was so precocious and so vile. But one of the girls, the boss's secretary, thought that I was quite remarkable and said 'This boy's got his head screwed on.' Anyway there were lots of these incidents which enlivened the dullness. The girls used to send me notes telling me to behave, to be good, and not to do this or that. I would then send back a note saying that I'd heard all this before. And so this nonsense went on.

It was an amazing place with lots of marvellous characters. When I left, I remember the secretary coming to me and encouraging me about drawing and painting. She hoped that I would get on with that, which I thought was terribly nice of her; and wished me luck with 'my studies' or what she called 'my studies'. I thought it a very grand way to talk about my trying to draw and paint.

Male Nude, St Martin's c.1920   AHT

I was then introduced by an uncle to a Mr Vintner, an engraver in Dyer's Buildings in Holborn. I started at two and six a week; and when this became unbearable I gave notice and it was raised to five shillings. Becoming an engraver is a very long process and temperamentally I wasn't suited to it. Again I gave notice and was given another two and six, so that the final break from Vintners was an effort because seven and six was quite an amount.

My next job was in Store Street cutting stencils with which one decorated coats. I used to design and cut the stencils. One was a floral design 'à la moderne'. I tried to make an intriguing and interesting design but it was all commercial – you couldn't stop and work out a design – they were drawn onto and cut out of a very stiff ochre oiled paper with a penknife, and then on this grey coat, where a stencil brush was used, there'd be perhaps a vivid blue-green design with yellow flowers. One had to do it as quickly and as easily as possible. The more quickly we worked, the more money the boss made. A very lively Jewish tailor would collect a great number of these coats; and the following day we would see them in the shop windows labelled 'Direct from Paris'. Runacres and I used to stand and rock with laughter. The situation was absolutely hilarious. While these paints and stencils were getting dry, I just walked by the window and picked up a scrap of paper and pencil. And on that particular day, making that little drawing was the thing that mattered. One was learning something then. All the other was nonsense.

White Face with Plumed Hat lithograph

There was a terribly nice man who worked with me at that time. He was a Russian émigré whose name was Gregori Czernek. And he was a very unhappy man, a disappointed painting artist and a lovely balalaika player. We would visit him sometimes, and he used to play the balalaika with great skill. He was a fine artist and later on in life, I heard him playing on the BBC. To us, he was Gresha. And Gresha was unhappy because Gresha was unhappily married and nobody in England could cook. All the restaurants compared to the restaurants where he had been were ghastly.

And Gresha used to bring his own sandwiches. He made rich cakes and he was very meticulous about the cake. Whereas Runacres and I had sandwiches wrapped in greaseproof paper, Gresha had this brown brief-case and very much looked as if he was either just going into or coming from the bank. An absolutely adorable chap.

We worked under 'Carl of Norway'; and poor 'Carl of Norway' was a poseur – even the name wasn't his. He had great ambitions to be a painter and used to exhibit at the RA. I ended up seeing him playing the guitar in the gutter at Piccadilly. I was so shocked by this that I just couldn't go up to him. He'd been rather a hero I suppose – this was a long time before – but he was a great favourite; and rich old ladies put shillings in the box. Then, still later, I saw him standing by a church, as a really tragic figure, in that what he had played at being had become a real tragedy.

The next job I found was with a marvellous couple called 'Fry' in Charlotte Street. The beautiful house where they worked has been pulled down. The old boy was a wonderful chap and his son a highly skilled craftsman. They repaired old Chinese screens and chests and every sort of lacquer box. These great lacquer screens and chests which I loved were made in the most amazing shapes. I used to wonder how the gold dust came about on these chests until I was taught how to do it with a vast pepper pot of gold dust.

Princess lithograph

Every night I walked from Fry's to St Martin's which was in Charing Cross Road. The cross-fire became thickest as a young man – indeed a very young man – walked across Soho Square, into Frith Street, Old Compton Street, turning right and just round the corner to St Martin's. There'd be an absolute cross-fire of charmers, all the way along the street. 'Hullo honey, what are you doing tonight?' And I'd say 'Oh I'm ever so busy dear'. Sounding absolutely ghastly. Then of course, you'd do the same jaunt down the same street and see the same women, so eventually one would say 'Good evening, how are you?' 'Very nice thank you.' And it was alright.

Mama must have been, in her way, fond of one – of course she must also have wondered about one, never having said anything about life in any way. But one day – this is really very funny – I think it was a Saturday afternoon because I was going to St Martin's in the evening, Mama said something like 'You're getting older aren't you? I know it's only natural – Mama used to say certain things like 'I know it's only natural' – but it does worry me to think of you walking through these streets to St Martin's at night; and you know there are – well there are, there are ……' I said 'You mean Mother there are all sorts of women.' 'That's it, they're not very nice women and they're…' so I said, 'Yes, don't worry Mama, it's quite alright. Every night I walk this way and every night lots of people ask me to sleep with them.' Poor Mama, trying for once to help. And Mama, in this sort of situation, saying always to me 'Well of course I know the day will come when you'll get married. I wonder who you'll meet.'

Seated Nude c.1919 pencil

Sometimes I would arrive at St Martin's life class and be half dead, having had an awful day at Fry's, perhaps sandpapering a gessoed chest and then covering the whole thing in light gesso. But from the moment I sat down and began to draw, the energy would come back. When I made this drawing, I remember thinking what a very fine person this girl model* was; and how incredibly lucky one was to be able to go to a night school where you could really look at the nude and sit down and draw. I wasn't over-concerned with portraying a model's character. And only to a certain point was I interested in the anatomical side. I simply wanted to draw what I saw. Models thin, fat, round, or square were all staggering to me.

Once I came in very late and thought I would be sleeping that night in the front room. I undressed, and there I was 'all nykid like.' I got into bed and felt this delicious warmth down the length of my leg. I was in such a state of desire and horror. I got out and the next morning asked Mama where the girl who had supposedly occupied the living-room was. Mama replied that having prepared the bed and placed a row of hot-water bottles down inside it, the wretched girl had failed to arrive.

*A very beautiful girl with blondish hair drawn, over a week, in the early days at St Martin's.

Every year there was a fairground on Hampstead Heath which was absolutely fantastic with its caravans and piebald ponies and Romanies – the women dressed in these amazing costumes. And marvellous savages with exotic features and great beads, beating drums and shaking spears in exotic and erotic dances which absolutely mystified me. And what really fascinated me beyond words was that later on, when I worked in Charlotte Street, I saw these same 'savages', two or three of them, as just negroes who were working in Charlotte Street.

'In The Beginning Was The Word' Illumination c.1920

I made my illumination – this burnt fragment – because I wanted to find out how they really got down to making these pages. I read about the technique in Johnston's 'Book of Lettering'. It was very simple. With embossed gesso, red and gold, you just had to take great care and have quietness and patience. The thing to do is to go to The British Museum and look at the originals, made by monks with tremendous religious belief who worked quietly away at these things.

This took a very long time and I used to work on it a great deal on Saturday afternoons and Sundays. Had I been left on my own, I wouldn't have copied it from the manuscript.

'In The Beginning Was The Word' stirred me profoundly. And in relation to the size and subject of the lettering, the borders are much too prim. Using the same technique, I wanted to make the proportions much wider and richer, to have borders of flaming colour. But my companions thought I should stick closely to the original – so that was what I did.

'Illumination' backboard, inscribed by Albert towards the end of his life

It's a pity this illumination was so damaged in that blessed fire.* What a tragedy it was. The kitchen table drawer was the only place I had for my work. Under this table, Mama kept a laundry-basket which she had a habit of going through during the night with a lighted taper. I can only think that this wretched laundry basket caught fire through some odd accident to do with that. As usual, I was the last one up to bed. And I thought I saw flames in the house opposite. I looked out of the window and the flames were coming up the wall from downstairs. The whole kitchen was on fire. I knocked up the boarders in their various rooms and meeting Mama shouted to her that the house was on fire. She took no notice of this but a moment afterwards smelt the burning herself. The base of the table-drawer was burnt out, and there were my drawings, just a soggy, blackened mass with all the water that had run over them. That's how I said farewell to all my very early drawings. My first childish studies of the Heath, and portraits of my brothers, my sister and Mama.

*The fire occurred in early 1924. Albert later considered that his mother may deliberately have started the fire to destroy his work.

Albert, Mother and Charlotte c.1920

Mama did allow me to draw her once or twice in those very early times, but in fact she could never bear it; and since we both knew what we knew, I couldn't bear to look at her with the penetration with which one looks at someone when one draws them. It was the most terrible thing and that's one of the reasons why I have no portrait of my mother.

I made the illumination in a room in Howland Street which I rented with Gerry Ososki, Barnett Freedman and Reginald Brill. This room was quite big and, like the rest of the house, panelled. The house had been changed into a warehouse at one time; and a window had been enlarged in what was our workroom, and turned into two doors that opened with a bar across them – to stop you from breaking your head if you just happened to fall out. A couple of years ago, I was going down Charlotte Street and I thought, I must look at this. I felt very sad. It was all gone, all swept away; and instead there was a concrete block, something to do, I think, with the Post Office buildings.

I remember very well one Saturday morning when the rent of seven and sixpence a week had to be paid. And we hadn't three half crowns.* Really this is very funny because Barnet who was nicknamed 'Socrates' at St Martin's and was considered to be quite a powerful, pugnacious young man and very argumentative, was not, in fact, as poor as some of us. Earlier Barnet had bought for some few shillings a guitar – not that he could play it – but he could strum on it. And I looked round and said 'Well, it's no good Barnet, it's ghastly for everyone but your guitar will have to be put in pawn' – I who was already long conversant with the pawn-shop because whatever we had at home was always being taken to the pawn-shop in Malden Road, either by Mama or by myself.

*For part of 1920, Albert is on the dole at fifteen shillings a week.

Barnet and I walked down Charlotte Street to a pawnbroker I knew there. Barnet was overcome at the idea. He'd never been to a pawnbroker and had such a horror of it that he refused to go in. And I had to take in the guitar. The pawnbroker took it; and suddenly I saw it go into the air as if it were on a trampoline. Then he caught it and went 'wham!' 'Seven-and-sixpence.' I said 'Oh my God, the rent's paid for this week.' So I took the seven-and-six he gave me in his clenched fingers and gave it, with the ticket, to Barnet.

I loved working with Gerry and he was a good friend. In an odd way, it would have been better if I could have worked on my own and then gone to night-school and had the companionship there. But what can I say? It was very helpful to have this room.

The first country holiday that I ever had from London was with Gerry Ososki, to this little place 'Dunsford' near Godalming. I'd tried to make certain drawings there and so had Gerry. My drawings have been lost but I can remember sitting in that train as we were nearing Victoria and thinking 'My goodness, what an extraordinary place, and what a curious thing it is to be going back to this huge town that London was and is.' I can remember thinking of what my home was and what I was going back to, and Gerry's home. Gerry was dreadfully poor; and the house where they lived in Rathbone Place was terrible. And as the train drew into Victoria, Gerry became tremendously excited and shouted 'Albert, we're home', we're home!' And I was able to see this, somehow as if I were outside this situation. I was of course excited to be in London again; and all that meant. But I didn't have this same upsurge of excitement about coming home.

Mr. Soft lithograph

The Singers 1923

This was just a small note and I was very moved trying to paint it. It was a step on the road. Many paintings from this particular time were destroyed; and more drawings have survived.

I did this after hearing Mozart at the Queen's Hall with Gerry Ososki. One hums the melody to oneself and obviously I had been looking at Piero della Francesca – those are the angel singers out of Piero's 'Nativity' painting in the National Gallery which I thought was the most marvellous picture in the world. Gerry and I listened to a lot of music together; and that's why I made a study of him as the flautist. He is painted in grey. As a matter of fact, it would have been impossible to imagine Gerry in a very rich garment. The one is a longing. And the other is just one's facts. By the way, when I drew these things, I never thought that a few years afterwards, I would see women wearing dresses again literally down to the ground.

Through this picture one lived in one's own world. One was in a serious lyrical mood. Those split wooden palings, the little wooden fence, this couple at the back with the greyhound and the crow, were all things I would see on the Heath and all so incredibly different from the life I was leading. I'm twenty. I think of this and of the whole life that one was really experiencing and living. And I think of what that means from a subjective point of view. This is a longing for order and dignity and decency and reasonableness.

Return to Holland

Albert & Charlotte in Holland with the Boeziek family c.1921

Oom (Uncle) Paul was chef on the Batavier Line which ran between Rotterdam and London, docking at London Bridge. In the early twenties, he began to visit 20 Constantine Road at weekends. He was an extremely amusing chap. On one occasion he saw a rather wobbly chair and, teasing Mama, he pounded it until it broke. She was furious and he led her into the kitchen and opened a bag full of butter, cheese and eggs; and made omelettes for everyone. We had a rather marvellous and unique tea. And the next day a new chair arrived. Paul would sing 'Pagliacci' at the top of his voice on tranquil English Sundays. And Mama, who was not terribly English, would nevertheless be distressed and embarrassed at this behaviour.

It was indirectly through Oom Paul that I returned to visit Holland.* It happened whilst I was working at Fry's, and I went over with Charlotte. As we approached land at dawn, I went outside after a sleepless night, putting a long grey overcoat over my pyjamas, and saw this very thin pancake which was Holland on the horizon. The captain and his mates, who were on the bridge at this very early hour, wondered what this lunatic was doing there. The thing I remember standing out about this visit is rather extraordinary. It's the amount of laughter we had there. Wherever Charlotte and I went, we were feted by relatives.

*Albert made his second visit to Holland alone. On the third trip with his mother, he was very ill in a storm during the return crossing; and vowed never to go on water again.

Jester lithograph

There was Oom Louis who was so funny that you could literally only put your knife and fork down and laugh and laugh and laugh. And his wife would say 'Now now, for goodness sake.' He was my father's brother and he had a tobacconist shop. He also played the piano very well. Some youngster would come into the shop for something for his father; and on the counter was a small metal tinder with a tiny flame so that customers could light their cigars. Louis's joke was – with a youngster or pulling someone's leg – to make this flame half an inch high or suddenly three feet tall. It was extraordinary the amount of laughter we had. The clowning the Houthuesens did then; and earlier, with my father as a clown at the piano.

I was mostly with an uncle called Bernard Boeziek, a painter and potter who was the husband of my father's sister Anna. It was he who took me to the museums, to Scheviningen and Zandvoort; and to places where I could look at the windmills which were then all in working order. I was taken to great lakes, with people in clumps fishing here and there. And to where we saw fishing boats going out into the North Sea, with marvellous old boys on them – some were well beyond their seventies and looked as if they were carved out of dark brown wood, with heads that were terribly wrinkled. When these boats went out, younger men would be lowering pails into the water, pulling them up and swishing them over the deck. And others would be scrubbing and cleaning. It was tremendously busy. And wonderful to see these great brown sails going out. I was fascinated by the heritage of these fantastic costumes that people were wearing. The fishmongers in Amsterdam going round with their sealskin caps. And the beautiful, very simple costumes of the servant-girls.

On my first trip I had a sketchbook; and one evening there was a little gathering of friends at this flat where I was staying with Tante (aunt) Anna and Oom Bernard. One of their friends was by way of being a fortune-teller at cards. I was absolutely cynical about this, but they wanted to amuse one and said 'Oh, let her set these cards for you.' And she talked away and talked away, and said 'Well I can tell you one thing, you're going to lose something' you know the sort of thing the clairvoyant says. I thought 'Well, this is a warning to me that the one thing I must not lose is my sketchbook' – it had the only drawings that I had made in and around Amsterdam. Then of course I lost it.

All the people whom I met were charming. They embraced and welcomed me; and I loved seeing them. But in relation to other things, Mama stymied everything. When I tried to talk with Tante Anna about my father she wouldn't say anything. None of them said anything.

Christ at The Column c.1921 ink and pencil   AHT

I wanted to stay on very much longer than I could. At the most it was little over a fortnight on each visit. Of course it was a happy time for me to be there and I was completely bowled over because there was so much to see, so much I wanted to see. But I was their guest; and I couldn't just go on being their guest and paying nothing. Always there was this business of my trying to draw and paint, and never earning anything. I couldn't say 'I am going to Amsterdam because I have enough money not to bother any relative.' And if I got to the point of hinting that perhaps, with a terrific struggle, we could both go; or the moment I suggested I might go, there were tears and 'How can you leave me, left alone here to do the work, younger sister, younger brothers.' One was literally tied to a post. Literally tied up.

Holland is very beautiful, but you have to be in tune at the moment with that beauty. I felt I had already been cut off for a long time. And I had already seen something of England. On each journey back, I again marvelled at the incredible, the abundant beauty of the English landscape. From that point of view, I have never regretted it. And also from my memory of Amsterdam, despite its beauty, you cannot help feeling the power and richness of a fantastic town like London.

What it really means is that there was nothing of significance from these visits to Holland. The thing that really mattered was that the damage had been done. Nothing could be repaired and going back couldn't bring back my father. And in relation to earning my living, I had to go back to Mama and London.

Verso   The Good Samaritan 1921 – recto, ink   AHT

Drawings like this are simply of and about unhappiness. They were made on very poor writing-paper and came through the paper. They were drawn at the dining-table with other people around, and I being quietly in despair. This was a study for a picture which was never painted but which became, I think, 'The Journey'.*

John, Charlotte, Albert and Charles, at his first Communion c.1920

*Painted in 1927 (P.78).

Vincent

Cone Hat II lithograph

My meeting with Vincent wasn't a sudden one. But the first time I was stunned by Vincent was at the Leicester Galleries. It was a Saturday morning, and I saw there two landscapes. They were so brilliant and so wonderfully vital that they gave me a punch on the nose. I also remember seeing there – and I've grown to love him much more – some things by Henri Matisse. They seemed to me, compared with the reality of Vincent, decorative and rather whimsical. In the profoundest sense, they still have that sort of difference to me; but that has nothing to do with Matisse – he's a wonderful chap.

I know that I was out of work and already going to St Martin's when I first read Vincent's 'Letters'. There were two volumes in English, and I used to read them by candlelight when this particular little room was not let and I could sleep on my own. They made a great impression on me; and gradually I saw more and more of this extraordinary spirit. 'The Letters' had an effect on me without one knowing it. You see, one lacked a father; and Van Gogh became a hero. Rembrandt and Van Gogh are at once so different and yet at once so the same. Vincent became a modern Rembrandt to me. And 1890 was almost as if I might have known it in relation to 1669. I can't tell you why I was so drawn to Vincent except that through his extraordinary drawings and paintings; and through the truth, and above all, the intensity of the belief he had, one sensed the difference between him and less powerful figures.

Albert standing behind Mother, John, Charles and Swiss boarders. Frieda is seated far right. c.1923

One curious thing that did happen to me was that I painted a winter scene of some peasants at sunset; and I was absolutely amazed when I looked through this Vincent book. There was a little scene of peasants with the setting sun – an orange setting sun to the left – which is very similar to this thing that I'd done. Certainly I couldn't possibly have known it, but it had an absolute affinity.

For years, there was a plaque in our window 'Board and Residence' in huge black letters on a brass plate found in the local market. Mama was very proud of this. Everybody had what Mama considered, quite rightly, rather common cardboard tickets with 'Vacancies' against the window, whereas this was a splendidly engraved brass sheet of metal.

Through some Swiss people coming, things began to be more reasonable and it was a nice period whilst they were there. They thought that they would enliven life a little for me at 'Twenty Con' so they took me to Hastings.

Straight Clown lithograph

Frieda,
Friends &
The Musical Hall

Albert c.1923

I was astonished at these great tall black barns for the drying of the sails. Everybody was terribly gay. And I, of course, had to pretend that I was terribly gay too, because it would have spoilt their holiday to have let them, for one moment, think that I found the beach incredibly painful on bare feet. I had to wear an unbelievable black-striped complete swimsuit from the neck down to the ankle. I think we had bathing huts; anyway the whole thing is, in I went when the others went in, you know 'I'm as happy as you are' even if I went in slowly which I did, I had to keep up a brave face with these other friends. A wave advanced and I thought 'My God, how magnificent this looks.' I thought 'If I can more or less face it' – everybody else did – I thought 'How can I not face this thing?' But before I knew what had happened, I was very nearly suffocated; and I completely disappeared underneath and struggled like mad to come up which happened. Then, at the second time of my going down, I completely lost control and I was flaying away, legs and arms making an immense amount of surf – my own rock. By the third time, I was absolutely in a panic but when I went down the second time, I saw a large fat man, heavily dressed on this summer day – I think he had on a bowler hat and an overcoat. I can remember thinking 'My God, what wouldn't I give to be walking on that beach talking to that man?' And the next thing was feeling Frieda's hands yanking me out at the shoulders and then at the head, yanking me right up; and in a few moments landing me smack on the beach with everybody saying 'What on earth happened?' I recovered with a 'Je ne sais quoi.' But for Frieda Schurch, I wouldn't be here today.

Frieda is standing next to Albert's mother c.1923

7th Nov 1975

Dear Sir,

I am sorry I am not able to give you more information about Albert Houthuesen. Enclosed I send you the last photo I cut out of my "album".

When I was at 20 Constantine Road, Albert was working during the day in a firm doing "lettering" as he said; in the evening he went to an art school coming home very late in the evening. So we have seen him only on Sundays. He was a good looking boy and he and my sister had fallen in love. Unfortunately Frieda fell ill and we had to return to Switzerland; my poor sister died of T.B. since then I had no more contact with Albert and wonder if he is still alive. Has he been successful?

I remember one sentence he said: "even if I starve, I shall still draw"!

Yours sincerely
Laura Hew

Frieda standing between Albert and John c.1923

Letter from Frieda's sister to Richard Nathanson.

52

Albert 'playing' the clarinet. Frieda dancing.

One day Frank Barber was at the piano – there were several others – and Gerry and I were at the other end by the piano. We used to pull each other's legs. Barber would begin by playing something in the manner of Bach or in the manner of that composer. And I would be the clarinet. It was usually Bach and if another instrument came in that was what I was, a clarinet, a flute or something like that.

There was this lull, and I picked up the telephone. It was obviously a man – a very gossipy man – talking to a very gossipy woman at the other end. And quite obviously by the conversation and the silences and the astonished 'No's from me, something frightful had happened – some catastrophe. Then the time came for this conversation to stop. You know 'I really must go now,' or 'The milk's boiling over.' And as I put the telephone down, so Barber gave that double tinkle of the phone bell on the piano. And it came in so beautifully that everybody roared. Poor Frank was a brilliant pianist and loved playing. He had a harpsichord at home which he kept locked up. He was one of these unfortunate fellows who had an 'anti Mama' in relation to music. Think of this. One day he went home and he tried to find the key to that harpsichord. He couldn't find it, so finally he said 'Ma, I can't find the key, where is it?' she said 'I've thrown it away.' The man just committed suicide. His mother had thrown the key away. She couldn't stand his playing. I think he took some ghastly thing.

The Beauty Patch lithograph

I used to adore going to the Coliseum or some other theatre. I was never such a film goer as many people are. I was much more interested in seeing living human beings, in watching some not necessarily very gifted dancer or clown, but literally watching how the figures looked on the stage.

It's almost impossible for this box with these coloured figures moving on it, not to have something wonderful. And that curiously has always interested me more than seeing a sometimes better film.

Town Crier lithograph

I adored Charlie Chaplin of course. I loved him when he walked along and was nervous or shy or was going to be bold or very frightened or bang himself into a table and send the glass flying. When he raised his hat with tremendous politeness to the viewer for the clap he had received for being whatever it was. But I didn't like it when Charlie Chaplin began to preach. I thought him a most marvellous fellow and at his best when there was just a subtle piece of mime going on.

I used to go to see and listen to George Robey because he spoke English so beautifully. I have never heard English spoken more beautifully in my life. The elocution of this man was simply fantastic.

Little Tich was a very small man, hilariously comic, and at the same time absolutely tragic. I first saw him at the Coliseum. He was marvellously and often grimly funny. I can remember him at the top of a staircase – there being no staircase of course – as a Duchess with a tremendous wig, receiving guests in a long train. Frequently, to please the guests – obviously a guest would make a joke – the Duchess would laugh very loudly. Of course no Duchess would ever laugh as loudly and vulgarly as that. And then this tremendous jaw would snap to. I remember a visit to the dentist where he was the patient. There was marvellous patter and dancing in these enormous boots. At one point on the stage where obviously the heels must have been hitched onto something, perhaps magnets under the stage, he would lean forward and the other man would begin to lean forward. And he would have an immense grin on his face, quite silent, just an immense grin.

One afternoon I was walking from Piccadilly towards Charing Cross Road. And I suddenly saw him coming towards me. The thing that struck me was the tragic head the man had, very lined and very quiet.

I think it was an absolute necessity for us sometimes to clamber into the 'Gods' and laugh like the devil. Nothing made us laugh more than Little Tich or whoever the other chaps were. Perhaps a couple of men who would come on as a horse. The first time I saw these things they were absolutely new to me. And it astonished me to see a perfectly serious ballet duet gradually turn into an absolute farce. It's really old hat. Everybody knows it. And people of course knew it then, but I used to laugh like anything. I was already making drawings of these things when I shared the studio with Ososki, Freedman and Brill. But

Magician lithograph

I'm sorry to say that through the certain inferiority complex that I suffered from and the criticism, none have survived. I may yet be able to make one which will sum them up.

During 1923, I left Fry's and began working for an architect named Aumonier, as a designer of lettering on stone. There must sometimes have been ten carvers upstairs. I was absolutely disgusted with the lavatory which was never cleaned – not that I ever used it except for 'numero un.' I brought a towel, soap and a nail-brush. And one day when no-one was there I absolutely cleaned the sink. No one noticed. One day they walked in and everything was completely cleaned. It got to the ears of Aumonier himself, that one of his char-women had cleaned this lavatory. Then somehow, through one of the men, he found out that in fact it was I and he called me. I was accused of wasting my time and told I should have complained.

For years I had to wear second-hand clothes. These were sometimes the cast-off garments of the boarders; but were mainly purchased from a second-hand clothes shop in Malden Road, where they were stacked in two great banks – the haggling and bargaining that went on. With underwear, I dug my heels in and absolutely refused. I was so angry that Mama relented. This meticulousness and tidiness was a kind of fear. I read the other day that migraine types are the tidiest. It all comes from this terrible restriction. All the time I knew I was wasting valuable time and valuable health in what was absolute rubbish. Instead of giving me the freedom to paint, one had to copy. Or the work was minute, like the engraving or this particular war job. It was true that it wasn't for very long, but let us suppose that in the meantime I could have worked in a scene-painter's studio, I might suddenly have learnt a lot. But that wasn't to be.

White Face, Starry Sky lithograph

The fake Chinese decoration on the chests was absolutely meticulous and minute – the others did the broader work. Beautiful old English chests were stripped down. I couldn't stand it any longer. It was extraordinary but it was all a lie to me. I am appalled when I think of the energy that I have had to spend on this sort of work, when, as a youngster, I was trying to earn money. And always with this command of my father's, this responsibility as the eldest of having to look after my mother and brothers and sister. That was always a crippling thing at the back of my mind.

Think of this situation where a man is longing to draw and paint; and goes in for a scholarship and doesn't get it. Goes in again and doesn't get it. And then again, until you're battered and you literally don't know which way to turn. It was through Rothenstein and only through Rothenstein that I got the scholarship. And I am very grateful for that and the opportunity it gave me.

The Royal College of Art

Aumonier's last words to me, the day I left, were 'Well, if you're going to be a painter, you'll be one despite the Royal College of Art.' Of course, I was at once quite overthrown by this extraordinary business of being at Aumonier's one day; and then suddenly finding, after this intense struggle, that I could go to the Royal College of Art as a comparatively free man.* I was so wild and overjoyed that the first thing I did was to grow a beard and wear no tie.

*After three unsuccessful scholarship attempts to the Royal College of Art, friends show a portfolio of Albert's drawings to Sir William Rothenstein, the College principal. Albert is granted an annual scholarship of £80. He is working at 'Aumonier's' on the Friday; and attends his first class at The Royal College of Art the following Monday morning, September 24th 1924.

The Day Breaks Not; It is my Heart lithograph

Stage Hands lithograph

I had to be at the Royal College of Art at nine o'clock. It was a hell of a business getting a breakfast out of Mama. It was far more important to get the boarders off than me. Nearly every morning, as I was about to leave, she would faint. I thought this fainting was real, so the morning would be ruined and I would arrive at one o'clock. It was simply Mama's battle against my painting at all.

Finally I was hauled over the coals and called before Hubert Wellington, the chief registrar of the College. He asked me to explain what was happening. I was very reluctant to do so. Anyway I had to tell him about these ghastly scenes. And Wellington told Professor Rothenstein, as he then was, who invited me to his house. I stayed with the Rothensteins for something over a month to give me a break from things at home. And of course all that was wrong too, because I had to call home and then there were terrible scenes.

I think that Rothenstein was the first man, other than my father, to encourage me. Well, one receives a great deal of criticism too. And the thing that one has to have is this demon in one – to keep going within oneself. There is nothing else. Finally it is like everything else in life. One has to be alone. There is no other hope for it as far as I can see.

Model c.1925 pencil

AHT

Today, drawing from life is considered to be nothing. I would say it's very important because it does make one look. And ever since that first looking, it becomes a habit. One never sees such a thing as a dull form. It's impossible after this first close examination. Forms are all amazing. It's always, one hopes, an intense examination, even if the drawings are bad.

It sounds odd, but I wasn't very attracted to the head of this particular girl.
It is a stupid thing to say. I ought to have been able to make something fine of it.
There was something rather unhappy about the girl too.

Albert c.1925

Rothenstein was a fantastic man in that he was known to and known by everyone who was famous. And his was an open house. I can remember the first time I walked into that house. The maid opened the door. I gave her my name and she walked down the corridor in front of me and knocked on the door to go into a room. As this happened, I had already seen on the right of this door, a wonderful little drawing by Rodin of a rather Michelangelesque figure crouching. And as the door opened, I saw this 'A Mon Ami Rothenstein – Rodin.'

Never having had, at that time, the idea that I should enter the house of someone who had shaken hands with Rodin; and to whom Rodin had given drawings as a gesture of friendship – that alone shook me. Being this work-boy, and always having tried to draw and paint, knowing that somehow I would go on drawing and painting, it never occurred to me, in relation to my schooling such as it was, and the friends and people I had known, that one day, not so far ahead, I would find myself in this world, seated at a table with Max Beerbohm, hearing him talk with Rothenstein about Henry James and Marcel Proust; and the old man – he wasn't as old as I am now – pulling Beerbohm's leg and saying that he didn't think that Max had ever really been bothered by over-reading Henry James or Marcel Proust. I was only just beginning to find out about people like James and Proust. And there was James Stephens reciting his marvellous poetry. I have never heard a man recite his own poems so beautifully.

The Bull – after Paulus Potter 1926 lithograph

The person who impressed me more than anyone else there was Ralph Hodgson. The first time I heard him talk, I was absolutely spellbound. It was an extraordinary experience. This was the first time in my life that I felt I had heard someone speak who had a complete and absolutely natural command of English. And who spoke with great authority. I remember afterwards going home and thinking 'This is how a very highly intelligent man expresses his thoughts when I stumble and go from post to post.'

On one occasion, the Rothensteins asked him to put their son Michael straight about the facts of life. This was after dinner, and Hodgson said 'Alright, of course I will, ready?' And he called the boy and said 'Let's come into this room, you and I will sit down and have a chat.' They discussed Blake, they discussed Rembrandt, they discussed Leonardo. And this conversation went on and on. And the parents were becoming more and more pleased. Then the conversation suddenly stopped; and Ralph said, 'Well Michael, careful of the girls, come on.' Then out they came and the parents both beamed.

Having listened to the conversation of a man like Hodgson, I then went back from Notting Hill Gate station to Belsize Park; and home to a mother who was full of how this and that was going to be paid; and whether art and poetry had anything to do with paying the rent. That's why it's difficult for me sometimes to talk about certain things, much as I would like to, in a more abstract way.

I had made a copy of a Daumier drawing, a very exacting one. And it was given to the Rothensteins. Max Beerbohm* saw this drawing and I was pointed out to him. He gave me a long, good look; and we bowed to each other across the room.

'Women of Algiers' - after Delacroix 1924 pencil

Cavalier lithograph

These situations, in relation to, for instance, being with someone like Beerbohm were unreal. This again may sound as if I have this whole situation on the brain. But in fact when it's a reality, it's no wonder that you get it a little bit on the brain. You see this little drawing of mine was made in that small room at home. And it was drawn in absolute loneliness and with great intensity. Then when something like this happens and Beerbohm honours me by bowing to me, the reality of my having to go back to Constantine Road and live the life there was so monstrous that I could hardly bear it. The guts of living was so extraordinarily different that it was sometimes very difficult to grasp what the world was about.

*A well-known caricaturist and man of letters.

Dear Sir William,

Thank you very much for your letter. As I said, it was a curious experience finding that photograph* under those circumstances. It interested me a great deal, and, strangely enough I had only just read his Picture of Dorian Gray. To me, dandyism carried to such a degree is a philosophy, a protest, a sign of genius. The one young man I know who has something of that same quality is Desmond, his beautiful drawings and paintings show the same exquisite affection he showers upon his clothes. But it has its dangerous side, I'm for a bare gaunt workroom, hobnailed boots and straw in my hair!

The first time I ever saw Max Beerbohm's work was when, as a very young man I went to the Tate Gallery and saw the series, I <u>think</u> called 'Rossetti and his Circle' with a wonder called 'Rossetti's Courtship'. Do you remember it? A bleak room, Rossetti leaning against the mantelpiece and a <u>cracked window pane</u> speaking worlds.

You will have wonderful models, and I envy you your steady concentration. Do what I will, moods overcome me, I have the chance to stay in a house in Sheffield and paint a portrait, but it can be torture to me. I saw Rachel just before she left Sheffield and thought she looked wonderfully well.

My warmest greetings to you all,

Ever yours,

Albert Houthuesen

Letter to Sir William Rothenstein dated 2nd December 1939. *Of Oscar Wilde.

Albert by William Rothenstein 1927   AHT

Through this household I was being educated. I who had had no education. And it was an ample household constantly filled with people, many of whom were famous and with whom one was asked to dine. And there was an ordered and ample table; and people sat around and talked. That house was simply a revolving wheel of the great. I don't, by the way, think this is necessarily good for a young man unless he is born into that atmosphere and can take it. And unless your Pa is able to help you maintain your balance, I think it can even be a bad thing. I just have this idea that if you are a young man with a gift for drawing and painting, it is almost better, from what I have seen, to be a rather lonely person and to have to struggle your own way through. Not to listen, as a youngster, to the conversation of what are the supposed geniuses of the time, where in fact a great deal of absolute nonsense is talked. You have only to read the poems or look at the drawings and paintings of certain movements which at that time were considered to be absolutely extraordinary.

Some years ago, I met a friend from College days and we talked about these times. I said 'Wasn't it all an extraordinary time?' 'Yes' he said, 'And I remember you, Albert, as being someone who was both ecstatic and completely distraught.'

Religious Woman of Antwerp (after Wenceslaus Hollar) 1926 lithograph

It was a very long time before I tumbled to the fact that Mama's dramatic scenes repeated every morning were to keep me from College. I used to arrive so late that there was no place for me in the class. And I would retreat to the Victoria & Albert print room and get out a box of various etchings. I loved Hollar's work and made this lithograph of the so-called 'Religious Woman'. They gave me permission to have the lithographic stone on the desk. I hid myself as much as possible so that this lithographic stone wouldn't be in the way. What a weight these things are. I used to carry it on my back; and I would have liked to have had it as a memento. A lithographic stone is a lovely object; and with the gum over it to seal it, it's like black velvet – very, very rich.

Hollar is a marvellous artist. An amazing fellow. We all come to England. The sanest country in the world and the most beautiful – said he, having travelled nowhere.

Follower of St Philemon* lithograph

I also made pencil notes after Rembrandt's etchings and paintings. And I'm sorry that those drawings have disappeared. I remember making a copy after his etching 'The Stoning of St Stephen'. The Victoria & Albert used then to have a rotating stand which consisted entirely of Rembrandt's etchings. And I used to go and look at those etchings; and whenever I could, I went to see his drawings.

I worked a lot in the museum. But I'm sorry to say that this was an expedient. Often I was so unhappy in the 'life' class at College that I had to get a new outlook. And that's why I copied the Hollar. A happy man would have remained in the life class drawing away like mad. It's such a dreary story isn't it? Fancy having to go over this again and again. As Mrs Bowen said this morning 'If it isn't one thing it's another.' It's such a ridiculous story – this finely woven thing of someone who wants happily to get on with his work but whose frustrations at home end up by making him more and more ill. Blake says somewhere 'The warp and the weft are woven fine.' It's all together.
Things happened at home which appalled me.

Mother, Charles and 'boarder'

*St Philemon, the most famous Roman clown of his day, appeared unannounced in the arena during the 'Gladiatorial Games'; and declared himself a Christian. The Emperor ordered him to renounce his Christianity or be sacrificed as a Christian. 'I am a Christian' he replied: and was martyred (AD.287).

Albert standing between Frieda and Charles (Charlotte is third from the right)

I was supposed to be the head of the house. Of course one wasn't so at all. With people in a small house sharing rooms – a couple of girls in one room and a couple of men in another – you can imagine the things that went on. There were other things, in relation to my Mama, which I can't even talk about, they were so awful. My God, they were a crowd. It was a miniature brothel.

The nicest people who came were these Swiss women. They saw what was happening and invited me to come and stay with them in Switzerland. This would have been the most marvellous thing because I had already painted a picture – an imagined holiday with myself and some friends, and tents for half-a-dozen on a rounded hill slope, then a valley, and mountains in the distance. When they saw this, they said 'Did I know or had I been to Switzerland?' Can you imagine my longing to go? But of course I couldn't because Mama threw up her hands and said 'Alone again. Who was going to clean the knives and forks. Who was going to ……...' It was all knocked on the head, every time. It's a miracle that there exists the fundamental friendship that I have with Charles, John and Charlotte. Nothing could break that. But Mama did her best to lever it away. She ruled by dissension.

Albert cleaning cutlery c.1923

There was the unutterably boring business of having to clean knives. Cleaning the boarders' boots was another humiliation. Sometimes I would clean the boots of certain men there with savage hate. Whatever came to hand was turned, if possible, into a riot.

I can remember laying the table for an evening meal and dropping the knife on the floor, then picking it up and beginning to breath heavily on this knife, then polishing it with great seriousness, using a napkin that was already rather tatty – making a tremendous affair of this, and finally getting a hole in the napkin and making it worse and worse.

Having done some of these chores, and through these impossible scenes of Mama's, I would arrive very late at College to find people like Edward Le Barr and Donald Towner quietly talking and demonstrating on the palette about the tone of the door against the light that was coming through it, and against the skin of the model. It seemed to me so esoteric that I could nearly have screamed. Yet they were right. It was the one thing that mattered. And to me, it seemed a world of abstract thought which really didn't matter a damn because I was dressed in second-hand clothes cast off by these hated boarders. And a pair of boots that were rather too large. Today it's simply wonderful. Anyone can, on the whole, go into a 'Marks et Spencier' and come out looking perfectly marvellous.

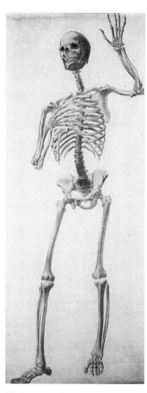

Italian Model c.1925 pencil  AHT Skeleton Waving 1919 pencil   AHT

This had to be drawn fairly quickly. Sometimes there would be minor upsets because the model wasn't posed well enough. There used to be terrific competition for the best place in the class. But it didn't matter to me where I sat so long as I could see the model. Marvellous some of them. Beautiful. There was an Italian model called Mancini. He was about thirty and his family were all models. They had posed for people like Leighton and Alma Tadema; and they took it very, very seriously.

One evening Mancini was posing and one of the other masters came into the room to ask whether he would have time for private work. He said he could have. And the master said 'Would you just give me a few poses?' There was then the most wonderful demonstration, to me, of one of these traditional models giving various dramatic, lyrical or melancholy poses based on the carvings of the great sculptors; and always in great sweeping, circular movements just like a ballet dancer. I remember being amazed and delighted to think that this master had come in. It was a marvellous demonstration of the model's seriousness. And I suddenly felt that I had been looking at something very old and traditional.

There were a couple of boxes, perhaps one for the foot and one for sitting on. And I thought it was straight out of Michelangelo's 'Moses'. I haven't got the original life drawing that I made from Mancini; but I've got the outlines of the pose and into it I drew a skeleton which I made up from various bones. I know that at St Martin's I had a skull and I think a rib cage, and one arm and one foot. Even in death, this poor skeleton was an absolute disaster. So Mancini lives in a ghostly way. He was a remarkable man. Very dark. Very Italian, with a fine head and a mop of black hair.

Seated Model 1923 pencil

Madame Paul c.1924 ink   AHT

The pose lasted about half an hour. Then a few minutes rest. Then half an hour. I don't know how these chaps did it. I should have gone completely mad. Sometimes you would give a model a pose lying down on a mat. And the poor thing would be unable to get up. Sheer torture I think.

This drawing of Madame Paul came about through a rest period. It looked so remarkable when she got up that afterwards, when she posed again, she was asked to keep that on for a few moments. It was very quickly and directly drawn and if there are going to be any influences then it's still thinking about Piero.

People at that time thought that painting didn't really interest me. But drawing and painting must go hand in hand. The man who self-consciously says 'Now I'm going to learn how to draw' – well what does that mean? Do you learn how to draw in five years, ten years, fifteen years? Painting is just the same as drawing. You simply happen to use a few colours. No, they were mistaken, and I find that when one is cornered, one pulls people's legs. Probably I said 'Colour is what interests you. I'm for the Chinese.'

From time to time, drawings were exhibited at College, with this insane business of cutting them down to get as many as possible onto a sheet of imperial paper. This is such a shame – sheer idiocy in these schools that fortunately they don't have today. It is cruelty – stupid to a degree. You can't see a thing like this cut down and living in this confined space. One was badly advised. No-one has any right at all, none whatever, to trim a drawing. You see fools sometimes put a dark stamp on a drawing and completely destroy it. The light areas are essential to the drawing as a whole. There's a beautiful etching by Jongkind of people skating which has been completely ruined by the damned fool who came along and had the cheek to put a stamp on it.

When this particular diploma 'Do' was on, the drawings were placed on this screen. I left the screen, and when I came back, they'd gone. The one drawing that I really cared about was a very simple, directly drawn male nude in steep foreshortening, like the Mantegna 'Christ'* which so moved and thrilled me that I made this drawing. It was without a single alteration. The feet were absolutely to the centre of one's eyes. And then the body went away with a slight curve over to the right. I loved making that drawing; and it gave me an absolute pang when I knew that it had gone. I can remember being very angry that someone had stolen these drawings, yet at the same time I was, in one way, quite aloof. Well there you are, I hope he enjoyed it and got a teaching job on it for the rest of his life.

Toupet lithograph

Another thing that absolutely shocked me happened at College when we had to do a course on architecture. This I thought was jolly good for everyone, but in relation to the time I had for other things, I didn't want to have to go to the V & A and measure doors – these beautiful Georgian doors, climbing up and down a ladder. I resented it a little. But nevertheless I knew it to be a good thing. And I brought with me father's compasses and a beautiful pair of proportional dividers in brass. The engraving on them reminded me of the engraving one sees on old armour. They were very delicate and very brightly polished, through being handled. Beautiful pieces. I can remember thinking 'How extraordinary, Pa used these and now I'm using them.' Come lunch time, I left these instruments on my board – I was a greenhorn because I didn't think this could possibly happen among artists – but when I came back the instruments had gone. I've often wondered since then who used my father's proportional dividers, and whether he came to greatness or to grief – this perfectly miserable fellow.

*Mantegna's *The Agony in the Garden*, National Gallery, London.

Supper at Emmaus 1927

For once I had to be at College. And for one week, I didn't care a damn whether or
not Mother fainted. I was locked up in a little cubicle, as we all were, and left alone.
That was why this was painted. And it is the only thing, other than those drawings, that
comes out of my college years. I'm only sorry I couldn't have purchased a decent canvas
for myself. It was poor quality board and cheap student paints. But one tried to make
something of it.

There were two subjects for this diploma *Supper at Emmaus* and *Charity*. But I'd already
had my boots given to me. This mysterious walk back from the grave is an amazing
subject. I couldn't have imagined a more marvellous subject. At that time everyone
spoke always of colour; and through sheer perversity, I used browns instead of greens,
although I know this was painted in summer time.

I started painting straight away on this panel. I didn't draw anything. I didn't make
studies. I didn't square anything up. You see the thing and you paint it. It isn't in any
sense a literal translation. I didn't think about 'Jerusalem' or 'The Walk to Emmaus'.
This is Keats's Grove which by then had all become overgrown. These are the walls and
trees that I saw there – the Dutch house, the sea that I knew. And these chairs that
I remembered seeing in Holland were all things that I knew.

These three are going to sit at this table. And whilst I was painting, I thought 'This chair knows it is going to receive Christ and so it glows with a halo.' I don't really like talking about it but I think that this is filled with the idea of a man who has come back from the grave. If you think of the immense robustness of some of the Italian paintings, this man has been crushed and he feels his way, just as these two discuss whether it can be the Master. And this table suggests an alter.

When one talks about philosophy in relation for instance to a picture like this, I think that every picture you make, every drawing you make, is a self-portrait. If they have anything in them at all, anything real, they must reflect something that comes from within.

Clown Saint lithograph

All sorts of things were said about this picture. Arthur Simmonds, a Cotswold sculptor and puppeteer, a kind man, looked at it and said 'You see the light and shadow you have on this head with the light falling from this angle, well that means this moon should be round the other way.' A fellow student at once said to me 'How have you worked out the perspective of those table legs? If it were right, then that back leg wouldn't be visible.' But to me, it was more important to make the perspective wrong for the sake of this piece of design. Afterwards, one saw this in picture after picture, really great ones.

People talked about Ingres a great deal. The reproductions on the walls were of absolute masters like Velasquez, Ingres, Raphael, photographs of Greek temples and so on – marvellous things. But if an Ingres or a Rubens were held up to one, as of course they were, it was always with the implication that there was something far, far beyond anything one could ever possibly hope to achieve. And true as this may have been, it didn't help. I didn't think about mastery of any style. All I wanted to do was to get on with my drawing and painting. One just tried to draw and paint.

I went to College absolutely thankful to have the chance to be able to work. But what I needed there was imaginative instruction. By that I mean you get more out of a student by giving him every possible encouragement you can. It's a very, very subtle business. One was criticised whereas life itself was a desperate enough struggle. It wasn't only me. I'm talking about this in quite a general way. It's a very simple and natural situation. Artists to be any good must be inspired by some sort of fervour – it's what makes a Rembrandt or a Corot or a Gauguin, a Seurat or a Monet – whereas at College, there was flatness in the teaching.

Had it been possible, I would undoubtedly have worked on my own. All one wants is a small private income, a roof over one's head and even two meals a day. Because what you learn on your own and through yourself is really learnt. A great deal of teaching can only be something which is not in true accord with oneself.

This drawing is through going shopping for my Mama at the Butcher's in Fleet Road; and although I didn't go into the cellars, I had the feeling there in these shops that that's what their cellars looked like. This wasn't entirely drawn from imagination. I must have seen cellars, I can't quite remember where, but I probably noticed the cellars in the grocer's shop where I worked and where the things were stacked and where the mice had eaten into the boxes of currants and sultanas. You see the butcher's shop was on the corner, and the grocer's shop was next door.

Walker's Butchers 1930 charcoal, white chalk

Catherine

Albert and Catherine 1928

Catherine

The first time I saw Albert, I was walking to the Common room for my lunch. And coming in the opposite direction was this extraordinary, tense, wild, red-faced, furious-looking young man with a spotless white shirt, no collar or tie, but I think a little stud at the neck; and in a black suit with white stripes. I thought 'What a man. What a good-looking man.'

Albert

I didn't see Kate there. The first time I ever saw Kate was on almost the last day at College when I was smugly congratulating myself on escaping the fate that most of my friends and companions had met with because they were all going to be engaged to girls at College. I was walking through a class room and I saw this quiet girl sitting alone and drawing.

Catherine 1934 pencil   AHT

Catherine

Albert drew me before and after we were married. I remember his saying, half-jokingly, that if we did marry there'd be nothing but hardship for us. We both laughed about it but it was a very awful thing to say. And we both knew that it would be true.

Albert and Catherine c.1928

Leaving College

Albert with Gerry Ososki far right next to Frank Barber and Donald Towner seated c.1928

The real battle of life begins when students leave college and they are perhaps already in love and marrying; and divisions come among old friends. To one person it's more important to earn money whilst with another, although earning a living is very important, he is, break his neck or not, somehow going to go on with his drawing and painting. That's the difference. If the whole idea of drawing and painting grips you, you don't think about making sacrifices. You make them. And you go without.

I left College in July 1928. And shortly afterwards, I began evening teaching at the Mary Ward Settlement in Tavistock Square. I also took two weekly evening classes at the Working Men's College in Camden Town. These were very light posts but a necessity.

I only went along and encouraged people who were interested. And when I taught it was in the humblest sort of way. If I made a demonstration drawing, I made it at the side, and only in relation to how I might have seen it. I didn't take my pencil and draw over his drawing as people who taught me had done. Every student did what he wanted and I used to encourage each in relation to what was his character and his particular gift. If it came to a leg too short or an arm too big, it didn't worry me. In other words, I always tried, in the simplest way, to let the student be himself.

There were all sorts of people attending, just as I was myself. There was a marvellous man at the Working Men's College called Seymour, who was a waiter – a very serious man. He painted a beautiful thing of a wooden mallet lying on a chair. I've often thought of it.

Albert c.1932

The whole thing about these two places was that the pay was practically nothing. And that year I began to do commissions for the Duke of Bedford. That was another disaster because 'Old Herbrand Bedford' who was a marvellous old boy but very dogmatic, insisted that I made copies of various portraits in his collection – not from the originals, but from copies of copies of the originals. My copies, intended for the muniments room, were made from small enamel miniatures which, to my memory, were very, very bad. It all had absolutely no sense or meaning and came about through being deeply in debt.

The most marvellous dancer I ever saw was Massine. But unfortunately I missed seeing Nijinsky. I've always deeply regretted that because in my bones I know that he was a tremendous fellow. I saw wonderful things like *The Good Humoured Ladies* with old Cecchetti as the dancing master. Absolutely marvellous. There was such a world of experience behind his dancing. I saw 'Le Tricorne' with Picasso's great drop-cloth and the original Picasso costumes which were really beautiful and full of vitality. He saw to it that the right material was used for each costume. Later, when I again saw *Le Tricorne* at Covent Garden, the costumes looked like black shades in comparison. And of course there wasn't the great curtain. I was stunned and overwhelmed when I first saw these things. And I should have been able to make much more of it. But I was already ill. And it is, to a certain extent, true that lack of materials and lack of space and air diminishes one.

Albert leaves the Royal College of Art on July 20th 1928; and takes two rooms in Savernake Rd, using the front room as a studio. That Christmas he and Catherine are officially engaged. He teaches at the Working Men's College in Camden on Tuesdays and Thursdays from 7.30 to 9.30 (from 1928 to 1938). In his autobiography *A Silver Plated Spoon,* the 13th Duke of Bedford refers to Albert's copies 'My grandfather had been made a member of the Zoological Society in 1872. It remained almost his only outside interest. It was he who took the lead in stocking the Park with rare animals. My grandfather's one venture into the arts had been to have copies made of all the dogs depicted in the more important canvasses against 'the masters' or 'mistresses' legs or skirts. Disregarding these was the least worry.'

Albert undertakes further commissions for the Duke of Bedford in 1933, 1936, 1937 and 1938. Occasionally he was able to use the Duke's box at Covent Garden where, in 1929, he saw the Diaghilev Ballet *Le Tricorne*.

Apple Head - Letter Home 1928 ink

You're the only chap who knows about this thing. If one didn't know, one wouldn't be able to guess. The drawing is a self-portrait. The apple head relates to the food parcel Mama sent me whilst I was staying with the Rothensteins in the Cotswolds. And the knife slicing off the top is my father's death. Mother was given, by a German border, a china figure of a German soldier which I thought was absolutely awful. The head rested on a metal collar and used to nod. This figure is based on that. Mother had a saying 'No news is good news' and in fact I didn't know what to say. The other young people were writing home; and self-consciously I made my greeting like theirs. Never before or since have I used the word 'Darling' to my mother.

No artist would have made an inscription like that* because if he did, he would have put it on the side to blend in with the design. This is a symbol of those times.

*This is the kind of gent Houthouzen fare would produce in 3 months inscribed on 'Apple Head' by a companion.

The Journey 1927   Leeds Art Gallery

It is an extraordinary experience seeing this again after nearly forty years. It's full of
naive faults but it has its own inner force. This land, this man and this going into the
darkness. Time hasn't been able to destroy that. The rider is full of foreboding and
melancholy; and is being led by an unknown man into the unknown. He is trying to get
away from something he obviously can't move away from. The rose is a similar symbol.
It is given in hope and taken in hope. One only flees because, at the other end, one has a
hope one hasn't in the place where one is. One can see the pools of rain water,
the reflections and the precipice they're going along. The Chinese costume of the guide
was just a fancy of mine – possibly a subconscious memory of pictures by my father.
By the way, this is a leaf from which the horse has just taken a bite. I seem to remember
drawing the whole thing out very lightly on the canvas with a piece of charcoal;
and then beginning to paint straight across it. Anyway, we'll call this 'The Journey.'*

*Previously titled *The Traveller*, Albert renamed the picture when, at his instigation, it came to London to be cleaned.
He also remarked that the rose in the rider's hand had been given to him by a maid at the inn below.
Walk to the Moon, Childhood Admonishment (reproduced on the cover) is the only other major painting whose subject
holds 'a rose of hope'.

Mountainous Landscape 1926-30 ink and charcoal

This drawing of mountains and landscape was completed just after a trip to the Lake District.* But it was begun long before I had ever seen mountains; and came about through my longing to know other places. I terribly wanted to travel and see things for myself but I couldn't. For someone like myself, Thomas Bewick, the wood engraver is a great master. And if he sends one into the English countryside, that may be better for some young English painters than going to look at Michelangelo. It may be much better.

*In the summer of 1930, Catherine's teaching salary enables her to take Albert and her mother to Elterwater in the Lake District for a fortnight's holiday. It gives Albert his first sight of mountains and inspires many future pictures.

Hampstead Heath

Hampstead Heath 1931

The one blessing when we left Amsterdam was that we fell into London; and Hampstead Heath became my countryside. It was a great, great blessing that I should have walked upon that marvellous piece of land.

I loved those streets that went off the Heath – Downshire Hill and Keats Grove where that extraordinary young man was living and writing those things. And gradually, gradually into the Vale of Health and up to the White Stone Pond. It is fantastic how clearly one had the feeling of Constable being there. And amazing to think of him wandering around the Heath. On that ground were painted some of the most marvellous paintings painted anywhere in this whole world – paintings fit to hang with the Rembrandts and the Michelangelos. An absolute genius. It is the incredible portrait he gave of where he was. It's a portrait of the English skies, of English lanes and fields. The portrait even of half an hour of some blustery day. I've always adored that particular and curious English genius that is Constable and Cotman, Girtin and Cozens. Terribly moving. A perfectly natural reflection of nature.

Self-Portrait 1929 pencil, black chalk   Leeds Art Gallery

My ancestry is mixed. It is half Dutch, a quarter French and a soupçon of Scotch.
When I meet Hollanders and French people, I feel absolutely at home with them and
with the sound of their languages, although alas I can't grasp them as I should – not
by a long chalk. If we had remained in Amsterdam, it would have been impossible not
to have gone to Paris. And if I could have travelled, I would have been freer earlier on.
There is no doubt about it that with the youngster who went to Paris and had remarkable
youngsters around him, they all struck sparks from each other. Paris must have been a
wonderful place for the young Picasso and Chagall. And in relation to that, London was
a very much more isolated place. But today, it isn't that any longer. It's an incredible
thing to think that I've seen more and greater theatre, heard more music and seen more
pictures and sculpture than a Rembrandt or a Hals. Compared to a young modern painter,
Hals would only have seen very little. But what he saw went very deep.

Albert and Catherine's wedding day

We were married on October 3rd 1931.
We found this charming flat at 20 Abbey
Gardens in St John's Wood, owned by a very
kind landlord and his wife. 'Utting' was his
name. And he was a grocer who painted in
his spare time. Sometimes we simply hadn't
the money to pay the rent; and that man was
so kind that he just didn't ask. I would go
down and apologise to him. And he would say
'It's alright my boy, I know. When you can
you will.' Wasn't it amazing to find this man?
Sometimes Cath or I would get a commission
and the whole rent would be paid. Then the
same struggle would begin all over again.

Celebration lithograph

Out of Work

I made many street drawings at this time. It was simply ghastly. There I was, a married man, quite unable to earn a living as a painter. I would have mad ideas thinking that perhaps if I walked about the streets drawing London types, I could find free models and also earn some money. Sometimes people would be amused and come and look at the drawings and at me. Sometimes they were very angry – apparently because having the time to stand and draw instead of earning a living, I was far better off than they were.

But you can't walk down the street, see thirty people, and say this one is worth drawing and this one isn't. I can't. To me they are all worthy. The only thing you have to avoid is a punch on the nose. Many of those drawings are of 'Out of work' men and were made around Camden Town. In a sense they begin with 'The stale bread queue' and when I myself was drawing the dole.

Self-Portrait 1930 charcoal, white chalkAHT

Lavender Seller 1931 pencil

If one speaks of experience, then I think the person – and it doesn't matter whether he's an artist or not – who has experienced certain things, must understand more than the person who has the genius to imagine. I don't mean that something can't be imagined with the utmost vividness. But you only really know what you yourself have experienced. In some ways you cannot unfortunately pass on that experience. You can suggest it and talk about it, but it's like a sketch of something compared with the personal experience.

Now that I look back, these drawings interest me because they remind me of what one wanted to do, hoped to do, and was actually going through. My misery was much like the 'Out of work' men I drew, only I had a mighty desire and longing to draw and paint.

When I went to stay with Kate's family in Liverpool, I walked up and down what was called 'Scotland Road'. There were these local women who, like Irish women, wore great black shawls over their heads; and out of these shawls peered their babies' heads. It was like a national costume in this particular area – absolutely marvellous. So of course, what could I do but try to draw and remember them.

Scotland Road, Liverpool 1932 ink

84

Beachy Head 1932

I knew certain dramas and tragedies of Shakespeare's. I certainly didn't say
to anybody then 'I haven't got a penny in my pocket and life is just hell.'
You don't say that but you draw a couple drowning on a raft. After an illness
I went to Beachy Head to convalesce for a fortnight.

I could only crawl around. I sat on the beach
and began to paint the sea for the first time.
The things that I made were very quiet and
straightforward. One goes to a place like that
and looks at the sand and the water,
the rocks, the horizon and the skies.

King Lear 1931 ink   AHT

Catherine returns to London in February 1931. That year, her two aunts acquire a cottage in Trelogan, a small mining
village in North Wales. From 1932 to 1940, she and Albert stay at the cottage for three months each year. In 1932,
Catherine loses her teaching post and the rent becomes due. After a year without work, Catherine finds a teaching job at
a girl's school. In April 1933, Albert participates with his contemporaries from the Royal College of Art, in an exhibition
at the French Gallery, Berkeley Square. He exhibits two paintings 'Autumn, Still-Life' and 'Interior'- and five drawings
'Market Type', 'The Paper-Bag Seller', 'Out of Work', 'Despair', and 'Heather for Luck, Sir'. Nothing is sold.

The Stack Yard 1935   Tate Britain

Wales

Trelogan became our honeymoon place. It wasn't just a thing of a fortnight or even of one year. It was constant. One's friends would jokingly say 'Going back to the same place.' And since we had no money, we had nowhere else to go. But it was lovely there. And through going back year after year, we came to know this amazing place with its colliers and farm workers; its marvellous skies and air full of bees and butterflies. I loved the countryside and I was in love with Vincent. And because one loved Vincent's work, it was an encouragement to go on.

To the Tate Gallery, 23 March 1958, in reference to 'The Stack Yard':

A wonderful landscape wherever one looked and in the village lived colliers who worked at the Point of Ayre Colliery two or three miles away from the coast. Painting in the open air near a cottage, I heard women singing beautifully, not snatches of song but complete melodies. I cannot tell you how much the character of the whole place and the people fascinated me.

This broken-down wagon was so beautiful. It stood in the stack yard of Owen's farm in Llanasa just below Trelogan and was entirely painted out-of-doors. When I asked Farmer Owen whether he could leave it for a while he thought I could paint it in half-an-hour. The half-an-hour became a week until he began to tear out his hair, poor man. But I managed to do this. The blacksmith's shop was across that meadow and I would hear all the time this wonderful 'clung, clung, clung' high-pitched, metallic, bell-like note of the blacksmith's hammer. I think that this was the first thing in which, in a small way, I was able to learn consciously from Vincent. But I've never been happy working in a conscious way from another man.

In the garden were tall rose bushes and a rockery made by Kate's father; and also a large and roughly made bird-table which would be literally filled with different singing birds. One stepped out onto the road, on the other side of which was the Afoncoch Inn. Above was a great hill called 'The Gob,' a name originally from Roman times. It looked south-west to Snowden and the mountain range covered in snow; and west to the sea. From the bungalow window, we saw this distance and the sea beyond.

Rocky Coast 1935 watercolour, ink   AHT

We watched huge rain storms begin to advance; and finally the rain beating against the window pains. Every night we would see staggering sunsets. The clarity of the air fascinated me. The huge cloudscapes and the stars at night. The brilliance of it all. Sometimes the moon was so incredibly bright that you could have read a newspaper. Kate and I would climb to various highpoints and look around at this huge landscape. It affected me very deeply. I made drawings and notes of the stone walls, the trees and the ivy-covered trunks. It was wild and deserted. There were terrific hedges filled with dead wood – they weren't trimmed politely as they are in well-governed estates. It was a rough make-do landscape and everything was very natural.

In the evening, I would watch the colliers walking back from the Point of Ayre Colliery. It was the first time I'd seen these fellows. They came into that village absolutely black so that until eventually I came to know them, and saw them washed I couldn't recognise them as being the same men.

Sometimes I would just begin to ask one or two colliers if they would sit. They simply laughed. They thought it was the funniest thing and disappeared into the Afoncoch.*

Miner 1935 watercolour

*Afoncoch pronounced 'A-Van-Gogh' is Welsh for 'Red River'. The local inn was so-named because it stood by the road above which the Welsh and English had alledgedly fought with such ferocity that their blood had flowed down like a river. Van Gogh's self-mutilation and suicide, also Albert's deep feeling for Van Gogh, make the inn's name eerily coincidental.

Miner 1938   AHT

These colliers were wonderful to look at. They all went to Chapel and sang like mad.
And almost without exception, all the children played the piano and were marvellous
musicians. I used to listen to their singing; and I loved being with David Lloyd.* He
would say one evening 'We're going to have a choir practice in such and such a place. I'll
take you along.' He had a little car, or we would go by bus, and hear these colliers singing
wonderfully – the very same men from the village whom I'd known on nodding terms.

When I returned to London with the collier paintings and drawings, I was at once
accused of being a Communist. A collier's is not at all a happy or enviable job.
It's a terrible job. But the reason why I drew and painted these men was simply
because, to me, they looked remarkable.

*David Lloyd was a famous Welsh tenor born in Trelogan, and the younger brother of the miner William Price Lloyd.

William Jones 1933   Museums Sheffield

To the Graves Art Gallery, Sheffield:

Late afternoon, walking down this summer white road towards Llanasa, in the far distance I saw a small figure black from head to toe walking slowly home up the hill towards me. I had seen my first collier. We greeted each other, "A Grand day", he said, and I thought how of all this brilliant day he witnessed a setting sun, and, later by the lamp at the Afoncoch Inn how he was whiter than a townsman. He was William Jones. I found a small shed and painted his portrait, for light I sat by the door, many came to watch, crowding the door until one could no longer work. When his daughter came to look at the portrait she said 'I have sewn different buttons on his shirt! ("Portrait of a Collier" Graves Art Gallery, Sheffield).

I recall this since it helps to explain things about the portrait you have and about which it is difficult to write.

I first saw William Jones coming up a white summer road. He was walking very slowly because he was an ill man. I'd never seen a man so saturated with coal dust. He wore a very old and worn suit. And the man, his cap, his hands and his face – everything in him as it were – was the colour of this blue-black dust. When he came up to me and spoke, I saw more clearly the whites of the eyes and the colour of the lips. The white skin drawn along the edges where the spittle had constantly washed. The ears were pink, not entirely coloured; and because the hands themselves were so black, the nails looked like exquisite tiny shells, except that underneath the nail, was this great half moon of solid black.

Miner 1935 charcoal

It was how he looked that amazed me. And I've never really been able to draw or paint that as I would like. I had no money to pay these chaps; and in any case, when you come home from the pit there's only one thing you want and that's a bath. William Jones was the first collier I painted. He was a quiet and gentle man and not long afterwards, he died of consumption.

Jo Parry

William Jones was a good man but he was very, very stern. You see that stern look in his face. He was that type of man who wanted everything done in a masterly way. He wasn't drinking, he wasn't smoking. Very careful with what bit of money he earned. He said he thoroughly enjoyed that sitting; and I'm almost certain that he felt like me. That it was a great honour to sit and be painted by a man of Mr Hothouse's character, because in those days, miners were looked upon as rats of the earth.

* Jo Parry worked with William Jones at the Point of Ayre Colliery. In 1968, Richard Nathanson visited Trelogan and interviewed Jo Parry and William Price Lloyd. Since no-one in the village could pronounce 'Houthuesen', they were called the 'Hothouses'.

Jones Whitehorse 1934

National Museum of Wales

Farmer Jones was convinced that the blue cotton wool wound round his left wrist prevented rheumatism.

Harry Jones was a good, decent sort of fellow. A very powerful young man and it was quite frightening to meet him in a dark lane at night. Through inbreeding and for other reasons, Harry wasn't quite 'all there'. He spent most of his time carrying huge loads of wood which he had collected; and that was how he lived. He wore other peoples' clothes; and when he came to model for me, he had on a false shirt-front with nothing underneath. His pockets were all filled with empty cigarette cases. The other thing is the ghastly alignment of his ears and the incredible hat, like something out of Peter Breughel. He looked past whoever interrogated him. He was a frightened man, reduced to this state through being retarded and battered about by the village kids, his father and brother.

For a time I was shunned by the village for having asked him to sit. First of all it was thought that I was making fun of him; and also, if I could take this poor boy as a serious subject, other farmers and colliers thought that I placed them with him. And after this I had great difficulty in finding other models.

Jo Parry

It's the image of him today. The only difference is he's grown fatter in the face. He wasn't born that way but had a very cruel father who kept banging him in the head and that's why he went a bit simple. Looking at it from that point of view, it's a pity painting Harry. But yet he could see a character in Harry.

His brother would come back drunk and beat Harry who would scuttle out of a hole in the wall at the back of the house. Everybody teased Harry but no-one let any harm come to him. And sometimes, when the brother returned and began to set upon Harry, his mother would run out of the house screaming; and men would come into the house and start beating up Harry's brother. He worked for the local coal merchant and carried sacks of coal round to all the local houses. If you gave him an old suit of clothes, Harry would respect that suit of clothes and he'd have 'em on for everybody's funeral till they'd fall ragged. Then you'd see him working in them. He'd attend every funeral no matter whose it was, dressed in his suit with his old trilby. And lead the funeral procession holding a small bunch of flowers. If he couldn't obtain flowers he'd pick daisies from the field and just before the coffin was lowered with earth he would throw the flowers on top of the coffin. Nobody objected to Harry throwing that little posy of flowers on the coffin. He did it with everybody no matter who he was. The poorest of the poor, or the richest of the rich in the village. He was the only one to do that. It was his last farewell.

Painted in a Village - Harry Jones 1933   Tate Britain

To the Tate Gallery:

I painted other canvasses and made various drawings; and always people came to watch. Then one day, I saw a really fantastic figure carrying a great bundle of wood on his back, and later this young man, Harry Jones, came to sit for the portrait you have. He sat four times, but now no one came, and after this I had great difficulty in finding other models.

A village funeral was a procession with the coffin on a farm wagon, but alone, quite apart and leading the way, in a long black overcoat and bowler hat, carrying a bunch of wild flowers which he had gathered from the hedges, was Harry Jones.

As I send you these notes I think of my long ago delight when the work first went to the gallery.

"May they come, may they come the days that enchant us!"

Yours sincerely

Albert Houthuesen

William Price Lloyd 1937 (92 x 40 inches)　　National Museum of Wales

Can you imagine trying to paint this thing in a tiny shed? Many, many times I used
to walk round with Will. Sometimes we would stand still and Will would say 'What
the hell are you stopping for?' There might be a marvellous tree-trunk covered with ivy
standing in a particular light against a dazzlingly white cottage. And I would try
and say something about this having an ivory-like quality. 'I can see bugger all'
he would say 'Come on, they'll be closed by the time we get there.'

I was taken to the Afoncoch by William Lloyd, but I couldn't drink as these people drank. I made no bones about it. And they all understood this. These colliers used to drink like fish. It was astounding.

If their glasses were filled and mine half full, there'd be shouts of 'He's gaining on you Will.' Then when Will had downed his there'd be shouts of 'You are losing I can tell you.' I used to stand the colliers drinks but they weren't interested from that point of view in sitting for me. The only thing was to make small notes because when you go into a pub with colliers, there's only one thing to do, and that is to drink.

William Price Lloyd

I was standing in my garden, in working clothes with my sleeves rolled up, just as Mr Hothouse painted me, when he came up the road and saw me. He asked if he could paint 'my photo.' 'I'm working' I replied. 'I'll pay you for the time you miss,' he said. I went inside his cottage everyday for a fortnight. When he was painting the features, he was screwing up his face, his eyes flashing backwards and forwards, and I couldn't help laughing. 'My dear Will, keep still' he said. When my four-year old son Donald saw 'my photo' he said 'Dada' and jumped at it, it was that real.

William Price Lloyd 1937

I enjoyed many an hour with him. He'd take me to the Afoncoch. The people weren't very clean there. 'My dear Will, I can drink,' he'd say. He'd order two drinks, but the glasses were so filthy that he couldn't touch his. And I'd drink both glasses. He'd call over and see us. We'd talk about Holland and the beautiful flowers. The butchers were just called 'Family's Butcher.' It tickled him no end. I took him to the Vale of Clwydd. We'd go for walks and he'd stop all of a sudden in the road and see a landscape or something. Can't you see the various colours of the trees?' he'd say. 'I can see bugger all' I said, pulling his leg. He'd walk about this village, time after time, and you felt he'd want to sit down immediately and start painting.

The first time you met him and came in contact with him, you knew he was something special, yet he always came down to our level. Whoever passed, he could see something special in that person or character. But he didn't say anything. He could see something in Harry. And Will Jones was honoured that Mr Hothouse could see something in him and want to paint him. The village looked up to him. And when he arrived word spread through the village, 'Mr Hothouse is over,' just like royalty. We used to think it was something great. I'd like to see him again. Everybody liked him. He was one of us – one of the village.

Jo Parry 1935 National Museum of Wales

Jo Parry happened to be one of the colliers. He lived down the road and we came to know each other. One day I saw him being carried home on a stretcher. One of the most pathetic things I have ever seen was this collier lying on a spotless bed, in his heavy clothes and boots, absolutely black with his hands and nails knocked about and cut. He'd been crushed between two trucks. After he'd recovered, I would see this extraordinary figure coming up the road. These colliers were all amazing looking; and some of them were just powerful hulks of men. It wasn't that one was more remarkable than another. But Jo was more sensitive. I asked him whether he'd sit for me. 'Oh yes, I will,' he said. 'But you must just let me go into the house first.' Then he would take off his top things and put on this spotless white vest. To these people I was an awful bore; and I knew it because not only couldn't I pay them anything, but it took precious time from them. I don't think Jo sat more than two or three times and even then, on every occasion, he used to doze right off. So all I saw most of the time was the top of his cap. We talked about all sorts of things. He was at that time making notes in relation to his attempt to become a lay preacher.

Jo Parry

Not living just a stone's throw away from Mr and Mrs Hothouse, we were very friendly. Then he saw me one day coming home from work, and asked me 'Would I sit for him?' I wasn't to wash me face, or me hands or anything. Just eat me dinner as I was with me dirty, filthy hands. 'Just eat your dinner and I want you to come up to Mersey Cottage for two hours a day for the next fortnight.'

I was started on a Monday afternoon from three o'clock till five. I was alright when I was sitting up, as I am in that 'photo' for the first hour, but once I started sitting down, I was that tired and deadbeat, I was sleeping and me head was bowing to the Queen one way and to the King the other. Of course I happened to fall once or twice out of the chair. Half-way through this portrait, he had a bright idea; when it came to the hour I was to sit down, he fastened me in his armchair with Mrs Hothouse at the back holding me up.

Jo Parry 1938

You see that cap on the angle. The young men in their twenties and thirties used to wear their caps at an angle, always with this dent in the middle; and of course we were trying to copy them – thinking we were young men as well. That was our way of fashions. That tally hanging from me jacket was recording whether you's gone home or whether you were still down the pit. Every morning you had to hand that tally to the man that was in charge of the lamp-room. You were getting up four o'clock in the morning, having your breakfast, walking to your work three mile and getting there by six o'clock. If you were later than that, your lamp was docked and there was no work for you. We were working from six o'clock till two o'clock in the afternoon - real slave working.

I was only seventeen when this was painted. And soon after I qualified as a local preacher. That sermon on the table was me very first. It stood out in my mind because I took that parable in real life. When I was struggling to achieve what I wanted I couldn't. I didn't have the means but the Prodigal Son, he had everything; and yet he threw it away.

A few years later, I was taken to hospital; and in that hospital, before I came out of the anaesthetic, I went through that sermon from beginning to end – every word of it. And the matron brought the nurses and doctors from other wards listening by the door. I didn't know anything about it until they told me. I couldn't believe it but it had that grip and hold on me life. I was trying hard to achieve me ambition but there were other obstacles. Me father was taken ill, me brothers and sisters were at school, others were getting married and nobody to work except me – something coming along the road every time, which at times used to make you feel bitter. But I used to get me pleasure in life by going out and preaching the gospel. And I do get great, great pleasure in it. If anything pleases me in this world today, then it will be tomorrow morning when I finish that sermon and come out of those Chapel doors and hear people saying 'Thank you Mr Parry for that lovely service.' Then I've achieved what I wanted in life. To do what I can, where I can and when I can.

Mr Hothouse knew what our circumstances were at home because he was one of us; and I suppose he'd been through it himself. And he could sympathise with you that way. He knew my ambition. I wanted to become a minister and I'm still waiting to. When he asked me what would I like as a gift for sitting for him, I said I'd like one of Dr Leslie Weatherhead's books – one of our famous men. 'It shall be done' said Mr Hothouse, and sure enough shortly afterwards, I received a one-guinea copy of Dr. Leslie Weatherhead* containing all his writings. That book was valuable to me not only in my line and hobby of preaching, it was also valuable because Mr Hothouse had given it to me and 'me photo' had been painted by a man of his character.

We had plenty of characters like meself in the village. But we looked upon Mr and Mrs Hothouse as something special. He possessed many talents. He could mix with everybody. Bring himself down to the lowest and the lowest and make them happy and enjoy them.

Young Collier c.1935   AHT

*Dr Leslie Weatherhead, born in 1893 of Scottish Presbyterian stock, was a radical Methodist preacher, particularly interested in psychology and spiritual healing. People flocked to hear him speak. He published a number of works, including a collection of his sermons.

John Savage c.1935

Jo Parry

By the profile and face I'm sure it's John Savage. I'm almost certain. He was a miner and he came down here to work when he got married. A few years afterwards, his wife got killed coming off the bus. Tragic. The features brings it back to me now, when John was young like meself. He died of a terrible ailment.

Barn, Berthengam 1934

I would spend hours on the deserted shore looking and looking and looking. One was absolutely fascinated by the constant changing. There was something so fundamental and grand and petrifying. Had I not been to North Wales, I would still have painted some seascapes, but from going back every year, I gained a sense of the marvellous space there. The width and distance of the horizons.

We had no regular routine but we rose early and Kate gave me three meals a day. That's a most important thing.

Woburn Matthias

'When Catherine was recovering from illness' 1935 ink   AHT

Cath lost our child at four months. We didn't have any more.
It was a very terrible blow. And a terrible lesson if you think that we had no money.

The Mad Sailor c.1935 pencil   AHT

How was one going, in this bitter and terrible world, to not only draw and paint, but somehow to bring up a son or a daughter? It was as if we had no right to have children.

This all sounds very odd and selfish. Sometimes we have regretted it but it is a very intimate thing. When one asks oneself 'To be or not to be,' one is considered a romantic. But in fact when it actually comes to it, I think I am a terrible realist.

Apples in an Old Felt Hat 1936

Catherine

For some years Albert had been suffering from a duodenal ulcer which we didn't know
about, but which drained his vitality. Also because we were both working, he didn't
eat properly. Finally he had a severe internal haemorrhage and nearly died. They didn't
operate but he had to lie absolutely still for six weeks, taking very little food.
This happened in the spring of 1936, the very month our son was due to have been born.
Albert began to paint again that summer. And in the autumn, he was invited to Woburn.
He shouldn't have gone and he was very ill there. It was a very worrying time.
These apples are in an old hat which blew off many times.

Albert

It was very much a reflection of the times.

When the Duchess of Bedford was killed in an air crash,* the Duke of Bedford thought he'd make a memorial. At that time I was penniless and owed over three hundred pounds. I could see no way of paying this debt because the work I did just didn't sell. Then came the offer of doing this huge window. The first simple little study with St Francis that I drew him, and subsequently every design, every figure that I made, was rejected out of hand by the old boy. He was charming and most kind, but absolutely dictatorial, on top of which, I didn't know that he couldn't see properly. Also I was ill. The thing was a mockery. Something that should have been and might have been noble was, through sheer obstinacy, sabotaged every day until finally there stands this monstrous wreck which I can't bear to talk about. With all the bombing that happened, that ghastly thing was spared. I wish the earth could open and swallow the thing. The irony of it was that through doing this, all my debts were paid.

In despair, I wandered into a room and discovered Audubon – an original, full-size complete edition of the 'Elephant' folio of Audubon's *Birds of America*. I very carefully opened this book and there I saw this staggeringly beautiful plate of the raven. I've never forgotten Audubon since that day. He worked like all reasonable painters do. To him it was a religion. Work like that and it's like praying.

Albert 1936

Memorial Window, Woburn Abbey

'He more or less went to pieces after my grandmother died. I had hardly been to Woburn at all since my grandmother's death, so I was interested to see the memorial window they had put up to her. It shows appropriately enough, the figure of St Francis surrounded by every manner of bird – I believe my grandfather drove the people who were making it almost to distraction. No artist's licence whatever had been allowed and all the birds had to have the right pin feathers and be perfect in every anatomical detail. He used to tell them that my grandmother would not have liked it unless everything was absolutely correct.'

*March 1937

A Silver Plated Spoon

Woburn Matthias 1936

Albert painting 'Woburn Matthias'

Woburn Matthias was on a chain attached to his ring but I was petrified. There was a little gate and I was always ready to leap through this gate and over the wall. In fact he just stood and stood and munched. Tremendous power. And I don't think this painting of mine conveys that at all. It was fantastic to think that the Romans brought these bulls over so many centuries ago. And as an idea, I painted that broken Roman jar and the oak branch which is a Roman symbol of virility. I was snapped by the rubbish I had to do at Woburn; so rather than leave empty-handed, I painted the bull and felt a little less ashamed.

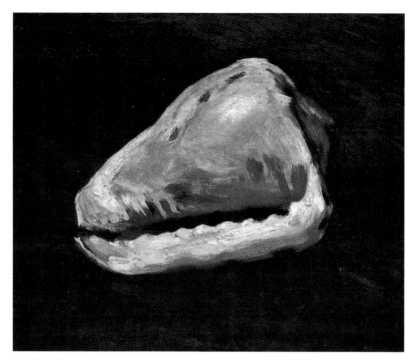

Sea Skull September 1938

July 2ⁿᵈ 1938

My Dear James,*

I regret having to write this letter, but various circumstances will prevent me from continuing work at the Working Men's College. I'm very sorry indeed, but I find it is unavoidable, and therefore tender my resignation. Could I have let you know sooner I would have done so. It has all been very interesting and I shall often look back on those evening classes, and the work done there. It is a long time since I saw you, I hope we may meet again soon.

Ever yours
Albert Houthuesen

Abbey Gardens c.1936 'Woburn Matthias' hangs above the mantelpiece. On the corner of the platform is 'The Old Felt Hat and Apples' depicted in the painting (page 102).

*James Laver was principal at the Working Men's College.

Convolvulus 1939 *I was mad about these peonies and convolvulus flowers.*

War

One had to work in every sort of place. And the first studio I ever had was at 37b Greville Road in St John's Wood. I was beginning to get over an ulcer and I cannot tell you how happy one was to have this place. I thought 'Now we are here in this marvellous studio – this big room with a whacking window – I shall paint a large symbolic figure, something over life-size.' This figure, rather ominously, was going to be of 'Winter.' But I envisaged not a grey picture but quite a colourful thing. The figure was going to be holding a holly branch; and I was going to have red in it, symbolic poppies and so on. Kate was posing when I drew this during the first sitting. Of course already one was very worried about the whole situation. It was foolhardy, in a sense, to start an enormous thing like that or hope to carry on because one's foreboding was of war. Yet I thought 'Well this is what life is and one must try and go on.' I drew it out on a canvas. But the sirens went and the bombs began to fall.

Albert c.1938

Winter 1940 (the bright yellow, red and orange were added in 1976 -77) 121¾ x 71½ inches

AHT

Catherine September 1940 'During the first air-raids'   AHT

Kate herself is a damn good painter, so the moment I said 'Darling, now we'll try and do this and you sit there,' I felt so guilty about wasting her time, because also she was teaching to keep us both alive.

Catherine

It was all an insoluble situation, and I was trying not to make him feel guilty.

Albert

Perhaps I will begin painting Kate; and the chances are that I'll paint half-a-dozen portraits of Kate, not only as she is now, but as I remember Kate when we first met, and I couldn't paint the pictures I wanted to. What about all the nudes? Do you think that I haven't looked at her waist and her bottom and her thighs?

Oh Darling!

Oh Darling. Well, of course I have. It's always when we wake up and Kate begins to do her hair. These movements, when a woman does her hair up. It's absolutely amazing. And what have I been able to do about it? Nothing – yet! So one has to live to be a hundred, and in the meantime you….. The thing I've noticed about Kate is her incredible kindness. I think Kate's had a bloody awful time being married to me. Perhaps if I grow old, I may be sad at my missed flights of fancy; but oddly enough I don't think so.

Yew Tree and Sheep's Skull (begun 1938)

I thought 'Well, first of all one has to try and keep sane. And the only thing one can do is to keep going with one's work.' I knew I would be quite unfit for the army. I remember walking into a barn on a farm in Letwell, called South Farm. It was a large barn and very blue and dark inside because the great doors were closed. There was a small window and another door on the south-side. On the ground, which was also blue-grey in colour, was a sheep's skull and a fragment of a huge yew-tree root which they had dug up. I just painted these things as they were. It was a very broken-up time. I carried these things around with me and whenever I had the chance to do anything I did. I just clung to my drawing and painting.

With his particular character, I can imagine a painter working away during a very terrible time. I can imagine a city is being bombed; and in his underground shelter or whatever it is, the painter goes on just drawing the people who happen to be there around him. Or being an imaginative fellow, illustrating a Greek myth – war or no war.

We had had the studio for eighteen months when, during the first air raid on London, that vast blockhead drops a bomb on it. The studio itself wasn't hit, but the adjoining studio belonging to my neighbour landlord Hardiman, received a direct hit. It was simply a miracle. There was a crater; and on the edge of the crater was our studio still with all the work in it. Mercifully, none of us were there. Whilst Hardiman and I were trying to recover what we could from what had been his garden, Hardiman found his top hat, grey with dust, and standing on a mound he put it on and called to me 'Still a gentleman.' Another vivid memory is of Violet Hardiman's piano keys hanging down by their strings from the limbs of a blasted tree. The roof of Kate's College in Camberwell, where we are now – may the Lord bless Camberwell – had also been on fire. And the staff and students were evacuated to Doncaster. Since we had no place to live, I went with them.

Sir William Goscombe-John, a neighbour in St John's Wood, and a wonderful old fellow in his way, offered to look after my work. I took over forty canvases to his house – all completed. There were portraits of colliers, landscapes, still-lives and one or two imaginative things, some of them going back quite a time. It was a very charming and polite house but after I left, Sir William went away to the country; and the maids thought that the canvasses looked rather untidy. So they stacked them in an underground corridor which was turned into an air-raid shelter. It was in fact a passage with a damp roof and it was very, very damp. At the end of the war, when I saw them again, the paint had literally fallen off the canvases. Dear old Goscombe-John had grown a great deal older, and one couldn't say anything to anybody. The maids were so absolutely stupid – their concern was to keep the place tidy, so as maids they were perfectly right. Only three or four things which had been placed on top of the others, survived. I regret losing these pictures – they are lost – but in one sense, I think, they are put back again in subsequent work.

Dead Sparrow Hawk 1939

Crown of Thorns March 1940

It is difficult to describe how sad one felt. One saw that the world couldn't possibly be the same and indeed it isn't. Very few people have any religion. And I can understand how it has gone. I had, even up to the last moment, hoped and prayed that there would come a point where he would stop these advances. One was appalled at the blackguards and the knowledge that the Hitlers and company were simply criminal adventurers in power.

The Magdalene's ointment in an old tin jar. The blindfold and the cloth with which the feet were wiped. I imagined that large piece of cloth as part of the winding sheet around the body. The picture is really black and white isn't it? It is difficult for me to talk about because I don't want to talk about suffering. But if you think that this was painted at the outbreak of that ghastly bloody war; and that one saw what was coming and also knew that one's life would be completely changed, then that's what this is about.

Albert and Catherine spend the summer of 1939 in a friend's cottage in Letwell, near Doncaster. The day war is declared, the friend finds Albert distraught, pacing the garden and saying 'This is the end, civilisation is finished.' In October, Catherine returns to London to begin a new teaching job at St Gabriel's College, while Albert remains in Letwell and moves into a nearby farmhouse. His mother and two brothers move with their belongings into the flat in Greville Rd.

Christ Mocked 1940-60 charcoal

Telephone Message for the Director

Mr. Albert Houthuesen extends his best wishes to Dr. and Mrs. Rothenstein, and his sympathies on the damage to the Gallery.

The Director may be interested to know that Mr. Houthuesen's studio has received a direct hit from a bomb, but that most of his work has been saved.

Received 6.25 p.m. 22.9.'40

The letters to 'John' and 'Elizabeth' are to John Rothenstein, then director of the Tate Gallery, and his wife.

Mersey Cottage
Berthengam,
Nr. Holywell
N.Wales
September 25ᵗʰ, '40

My Dear John,

Just a short note.

We found your letter here on our return after a hellish week in London. Very glad to hear you are both well. The studio is no more, though it looks normal from the street.

Poor Hardiman's place is completely demolished, mercifully none of us were there at the time.

Although we've been shifting things for a week, I still find it difficult to realise one's life there is finished.

Every best wish, and our love to you both,
Ever yours,
Albert

The few pieces of silver we had were stolen!

Christ Mocked 1939 ink

Mersey Cottage

My Dear John and Elizabeth,

I do hope you are both well. The news on the wireless is very disturbing. It's a little more peaceful in this particular spot but they fly right over and at night one can see the bombing of L'pool. We saw a German bomber chased and heard afterwards that it had been brought down.

If you have a moment just send us a postcard so that we may know how you are.

All my love,
Albert

The Apple Branch   Inscribed on verso: *Trelogan November 1940, shop Newydd above the baker.*

It was an extraordinary thing walking about these fields and hearing the sirens wailing. I remember William Lloyd saying to me 'What's going to happen to you now Albert?' I said 'I just don't know.' I didn't, in relation to what I might be doing. William Lloyd and the colliers were all very moved by the war – everybody was – but they knew their lives would go on exactly as before because it was essential that these collieries be kept going.

I bought that glove from a hedge-cutter in Yorkshire. He was an irascible old boy who used to work like a fury clearing these hedges and ditches.

One terrifying, very dark night, there were sudden incredibly brilliant flashes of light as the bombs fell and the sky became red. In the same country road, where I happened to be standing, were young men and women making love and fooling around. It was extraordinary to see this terrible burning and think of what was going on over the other side of the river. And then to see lovers running up and down the street playing 'Touch' and disappearing into the hedges.

This picture is, to me, a symbol of what one was going through. Of the world being torn to pieces. Heaven knows it's mildly put.

*Catherine temporarily moves to Leicester with her college. Albert remains in Trelogan where, in November, during the bombing of Liverpool, he begins painting 'The Apple Branch'. In December, Catherine's college moves to Doncaster.

I was rejected from the army on health grounds. I was no good – Grade IV, the lowest I believe. I was examined in Mansfield and there we all were, around fifty men, with just our trousers and shoes on. I was shocked to see how pathetic this man looked, and how old that one looked. And what a gnarled, emaciated worker, or what a tough, powerful young man or a broken man this one looked. Then to realize that this extraordinary, motley crew of men were all born in the same year, really put the wind up me.

I began *Voyage* in St John's Wood and carried on in Letwell, Loversall, Tickhill, Chatham Street, Oxted; and then finally here where the shell and convolvulus were painted.

Working on it again and again, even sometimes during a migraine, helped to keep me sane. The magnolias against the blue were the first things I painted. It wasn't changed in a large way, but in such small, subtle things, all the time, which made a great difference. I like the way the title is in French as it is in English. This magnolia is beginning to open. This one is more fully open. This one is really open. And this one is going. The figure 'Fate' carries out these shapes. A picture like this has its own law and these shapes make themselves.

Before my medical examination, I had thought it would be a marvellous idea if I could be employed in drawing and painting colliers. I wrote a letter of application, in relation to being a war artist, saying the chances were that I wouldn't be fit enough for the army. I was invited to bring along a portfolio and the next thing I heard was, as usual, 'Dear Sir, We regret………….'

Voyage 1940-54

AHT

When we moved to Letwell, I had to register at the Worksop Labour Exchange. And there I was an absolute problem. They were very nice chaps but nobody knew what to do with me. I was offered various jobs and from a physical point of view, I was unable to tackle any. One was a boiler-man at the Worksop hospital. Another was to be a farm labourer – I rather liked that idea. The next thing I was offered was to be a collier at Langold pit which was near Letwell. I was questioned by a marvellous works manager who came to the conclusion, as it was with most things, that I would be a hopeless collier and wouldn't be able to dig out one decent lump of coal. But he thought it might be a good idea if I worked on the surface sorting coal on a belt. I didn't know this but apparently great heaps of coal did come down and along a belt and had to be sorted. He was a wonderfully humourous fellow, and a very down to earth and practical man. We talked this over and then he said 'No, but I've got it – the telephone exchange, with a cultured voice like that.' I went back that afternoon to the cottage and I said to Kate 'Well, I'm going to try and be a telephonist.' I could see myself with this mouthpiece and an earphone doing this marvellously, clutching plugs and connecting all the wrong people to all the wrong people. Anyway the telephone exchange came to nothing.

It was all somewhat fantastic. I had suddenly found myself in this odd situation of wanting to help and being quite unable to do these things. The long and short of it was that I was sent to the Doncaster Engineering Works of the London North Eastern Railway (L.N.E.R), and was interviewed by a Mr. Windle who was the head draughtsman.

He questioned me about drawings and what I knew about engineering and locomotives. Of course I knew nothing about locomotives. It was the absolute devil, everything I touched, I didn't know anything about. Anyway I think I just missed being an engine driver and was taken on as a tracer in the Drawing Office of the L.N.E.R.

Acrobat Clown lithograph

Punch Drunk Bruiser lithograph

Laurelled Head 1941 charcoal

The Farm House
c/o Mrs. Burnet,
Loversall
Nr Doncaster
Nov. 11ᵗʰ '41

My dear Elizabeth,

I ought to write you a long letter, describing 'The New Life' at great length, but that wonderful document must be left until a later day, this is just a wink, a handshake in a crowded room! I'm a success, would you believe it, I'm a success. I've worked at the L.N.E.R. Locomotive drawing office for over a month, and I'm a success. The first week was a bit trying, but, Mama Stavin, I'm rolling it! My companions are charming men, and have been very helpful. I hope it won't be very long before you see <u>really</u> remarkable engines on the lines. I don't guarantee that they will go mind you, but they'll be amazing!

One thing this job has done for me. I now see clearly how I would decorate a booking-hall like the Doncaster building. And I believe the public would be interested, and see decorations they haven't seen before, and the railway people would be interested, I mean those who really know about all the work that goes on, and which is so fascinating, and so truly romantic. But I seem to be born to complete these things in vision, to make them absolutely real, but only for myself. Well, we shall see what happens.

Christ Mocked 1941 charcoal

I've had to move I'm sorry to say, the cottage was charming, but the journey was too much. I had to get up at 6.30 to get to work at 9, and getting soaked with rain sometimes walking to Langold wasn't pleasant. It's curious looking back to the cottage now, it already seems long ago, which I suppose is because one's life is so different now.

We are lucky, for the people here are charming.

One day when you have a moment write to me, and tell me about yourself and John. I hope you are both very well.

Goodbye,

Ever yours,

Albert

Cath sends her love.

P.S. What about the progress of the book on Stanley?[*]

*Spencer

Dec 2ⁿᵈ, 1941

*The Farm House,
Loversall*

My Dear John,

Many thanks indeed for your letter with its delightful news. It was there when I returned from the 'office' and is a great encouragement. Cath goes to London Thursday I think and will take the picture and a 'hedge' drawing which I think you liked. Do you think £10 would be alright (framed of course!).

Sometimes I am able to look over the 'works' and there are the most wonderful subjects everywhere. I long to paint them, and hope I may do so one day. Marvellous themes, and no one seems to me to have really said anything about it yet.

Again, many many thanks and a salutation to you both.

*Ever yours,
Albert*

White Face, Black Necktie lithograph

During the war, the Government assumed control of the independent railway companies. Production at the railway workshops was no longer confined to the construction of new locomotives and rolling stock; but extended to the conversion of old rolling-stock into ambulance trains (290 were converted at Doncaster and York in 1942); and the manufacture of aeroplane parts, tank hulls, gun-carriages, armour-plating and periscope parts. Many new workers were taken on during the war; and the more experienced were moved around to help the war-time workers.

The Plant

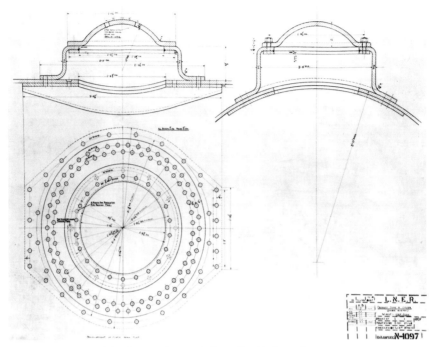

Inscribed, initialled and dated *Pressed Dome & Cover (Double Riveted) AH 15.1.43*

I can't tell you how odd I felt at tracing boilers and locomotives in sections – plans of these bogies, every sort of thing, things that were marvellously beautiful in themselves but which I could find no way, at that time, of using because at the end of the day, I was completely whacked. There is a way of keeping calm and making a beautiful tracing technically, but since I couldn't read the drawings and wasn't a good tracer, I went to the chief engineer to ask whether I might work in the workshop. This was a huge place where these locomotives were being cleaned and moved down great sheds on cranes that were slung from the roof.

In this dimly-lit workshop were boys with enormous aprons working at braziers which looked literally like pails with pierced holes in them, heating these particular metal parts. And overhead, a great locomotive was slowly being moved along and then lowered. Well, it was wonderful and I thought 'My God! If only I could get my teeth into this and do something about drawing and painting it, I could give the lot to the Plant; and at least it wouldn't be completely wasting my time.' But when I asked for permission to do this, one just met with a blank wall. There was nothing doing.

The men I worked with were very surprised that I came there and settled down immediately, even joining the Trade Union voluntarily. I was told by them that art compared with building railways was unimportant. I pointed out to them that when you draw a diagram of a locomotive on paper – the moment something is on paper – it's inaccurate. They were also flummoxed by perspective and didn't realise that tracing had nothing to do with how one designs a picture. I remember a furious argument about whether a table was or was not flat; and their reply being 'By God, this man's got gift of gab.'

R. Nathanson Esq.

British Railways Board,
(Traction & Rolling Stock) Dept
Office of Director of Design
26ᵗʰ April, 1968

Dear Sir,

Thank you for your letter of the 15ᵗʰ April. All the staff records relating to the period of Mr Houthuesen's employment have been destroyed, but I have managed to salvage the entry in the Post Book which shows the period he was employed at Doncaster.

The only time a Railway Draughtsman could be called upon to show any artistry is when he is preparing for perspective views of rolling stock etc. The two drawings in question are purely mechanical engineering drawings and cannot be classed as artistic in any way.

Yours faithfully,
W.G. Jowett

Busker with Dog lithograph

Doncaster was filled with all sorts of places and eventually I discovered a wonderfully old-fashioned dining-room run by a bald-headed man of about fifty with an enormous golden retriever running around. A very nice old boy and also there was a charming girl who was waitress there. These people were kindness itself. They used to serve fifty or sixty people at lunchtime. One Saturday I was in Doncaster for the afternoon because there was a market-place which was interesting; and I passed this dining-room. A big, powerful-looking labourer came out with a great sack on his back, and a moment afterwards the proprietor came out weeping. He said to me 'Did you see the ....?' I knew at once what he meant. He said 'It's my dog, it's dead.' And the poor old boy burst into tears. I went back with him into this little shop where this marvellous, large, beautiful dog had just died. And he broke down and said 'You'll think I'm an awful old fool won't you?' I said 'Of course I don't, as if I would think that.' But I remember all sorts of wonderful people there.

In 1942, Albert and Catherine move to Loversall. Then, nine months later, to a guest-house in Tickhill village. In summer 1943, they rent a cottage for £1 a week. Albert works two hours' overtime, four evenings a week; with fire-practice and work on Saturday mornings until midday. Because of the distance to work, also his health, Albert discontinues overtime.

Dear Mr Nathanson,

The Drawing Offices at Doncaster works were situated on the top floor of a long two storey building facing the main lines and overlooking the station. They were part of the original works built in 1850.

The offices consisted of carriage and wagon department in one half and the locomotive Department in the other – each about 300 feet long by 60 feet wide and independent of each other though both under the chief mechanical engineer who in Albert's time was …., a most unpopular man. ……When the war came we all found ourselves in reserve occupations and with so much war work………Four lady tracers appeared. . ……Well we had hardly recovered from the feminine invasion of our monastic calm when of all things a male tracer appeared and to our horror an artist!

While we were resigned to the lady tracers and in fact came to enjoy their presence, a male tracer was a different matter. By our training I think we were essentially practical and the very word 'Art' was something for the 'Dilettantes' and long-haired types (the last hardly applies now). I dare say Albert felt a bit uncomfortable at first coming into such a closed community where every technical discussion must have been meaningless to him. I hope we did not show our feelings too obviously…..

Discipline was very easy and one could always go and chat to a colleague so long as the gossip was not too prolonged. As I remember it, Albert did not leave his board very much – we went either to help or chat about a painting of which we knew nothing. It was on one of these occasions when I was standing at his board that he drew my attention to the steely quality of the light shining from the clouds on the wet slates of the roofs of some of the houses on the other side of the station. We were looking across the office and through the windows on the opposite side. For some peculiar reason Albert seemed to stamp this view on my mind! On the occasion of a little Art exhibition in Doncaster several of us went to see the painting Albert was showing. So far as I remember it was something like the sketch enclosed. We were not impressed! And we ragged him about the handles which we did not think were opposite one another. It didn't get him down. I don't think anybody won any of these arty arguments – both sides remained unconvinced. Mrs Houthuesen showed a subject 'Bindweed' which we thought much better than Albert's.

I enclose a rough plan of the office as it was during the war. It was about 300 feet long by 60 feet wide. The light was somewhat reduced by the black out. All the side windows at Albert's side were painted black and also the roof lights so that things were not at their best during his stay with us. Incidentally, scrap tracings if not too damaged made reasonable handkerchiefs after washing out the ink and hemming. This was a consideration when clothing coupons were in use. I expect Albert was wise to this.

Yours sincerely,

B.E.Squires

I was doing my bit to defend the east coast of England. One evening there was an alarm and we all had to rush out and take up certain positions. I thought that this was so unbelievably funny because we all rushed to these posts, each with his rifle, supposedly to shoot down the parachutists who were falling thick and fast on Yorkshire; and there was not a single loaded rifle among us. The only man who could really shoot was a farmer's boy who had spent all his life shooting crows. He was terrific with a rifle; and at practice targets he'd simply take a rifle, set it up, and go bang, bang, bang, one after the other – straight in the middle. And we used to go bang, bang, bang – no mark at all.

Hubbub lithograph

On one occasion, we were given ammunition for target practice and I said 'I can't shoot' but was told to go ahead. I lay down, went bang – bull's eye. This was simply because I thought 'the bullet curves like that and if I wobble this rifle about too much it won't hit anything, but if I hit this quickly……..' Well, nobody else had this bull's eye and after this they insisted that I was a good shot. But I said 'I'm not, I'm not. I assure you it was an accident.' They said 'Liar, again. Do it again.' And I did it again, bang – nowhere, not a single mark on anything. Then the chief said 'It's all very well you're fooling about like this but on Sunday morning you are in the team against this other team.' I said 'I can't.' 'Oh, the hell with you.' So we all lay down, our little crowd, and went bang, bang, bang, bang. And hit nothing. Then the next team went bang, bang, bang, and they all had bull's eyes. They were all farmers' boys.

24.2.68

Dear Mr Nathanson,

Albert's tracings were mostly replacements for existing locomotive detail parts, the tracing of which were badly worn through frequent use. I don't think he did any of the new work. I seem to have given you a wrong impression of the war work. We did not produce any of the designs in our office. Sets of tracings or prints were supplied by the Government departments concerned or by other railway offices and also private firms. The master copies were of course kept in the office and keeping them up to date was quite a job as there were so many modifications especially on those supplied by the Government ministries. Sometimes it was easier to retrace the drawings completely than to add all the alterations or alternatives…….

Yours sincerely

B.E.Squires

Three Years Hell 1944 watercolour   AHT

In all great government works, where thousands of men are employed, much time is lost in doing nothing. I felt that what was supposed to be help was ineffectual marking time. And in relation to this ghastly business of what is called 'winning a war' it was all a negation. Around me I saw going on what was, unconsciously in many ways, a vast sabotage all the time. One day, you would hear that so many carriages or rolling-stock had gone, newly upholstered by super craftsmen, into such a yard, and that some particular night-shift of workers with a grudge about something had slept in them and then ripped up the seats with their knives. In the office was a shop steward; and instead of spending about an hour a day attending to union business, he spent the whole of the day walking up and down this office filling in forms and getting forms filled in by other members. Well, to me, all these things were losing the war, not helping to win it. But one was in a hateful position anyway. I was just a number and I got on with all these things.

The people I worked with weren't bad chaps but they couldn't change anything. And eventually I think they must have seen that I thought a great deal of it was humbug, just as so called 'over-time' over these tracings didn't really make a terrific difference.

The men in the office had spent their whole lives in these beliefs about accuracy. Despite all my love of painting and drawing and my beliefs, I was, at the end almost accepting their views; and I was literally mad. One day a colleague came to my desk and said something like 'What's happening. Now what are you going to do?' I took a sheet of white paper about nine by twelve inches, I had a pencil in my hand, I was absolutely frantic, and I dug into this paper the head of a madman with hair flying and I said 'Look, this is what I am now.'

Christ Mocked 1943 charcoal

My dear Elizabeth,

    Thank you very much for your kind and encouraging letter. I was very sorry to hear that you have been ill and I do hope you are really well again.

I was rather knocked out too and was away from the office for some time, and when I began to recover I did the drawing you have with one or two others.

Your letter cheers me. I don't think painters need criticism, not really, if they are any good they'll do that, but they do need encouragement for that's a real help, and certainly you do that for me.

I don't think I shall forget these past four years. Through a lack of cynicism I was never one to jostle, and it's curious what one learns. It would need a long letter to describe *what I have felt, and in any case it doesn't matter, but to paint it, that matters very much <u>to me</u> and the seemingly eternal denial is at times almost unbearable. My whole life I have tried hard to be a painter, but the time spent with a brush in my hand is nothing compared to the idiotic mountains I have been fated to shovel away.*

With regard to your question I hope it will not be long before we can meet and talk about these things. I feel I would rather do that than write about them.

I can see from time to time I shall have to send you a drawing or a painting for the selfish joy of receiving a letter of encouragement from you.

Goodbye my dear,

With all good wishes,

Albert

It sounds a bitter thing to say, but I think it is true that it would have been more amusing if, during that period, I had been in prison where at least they might have said 'This idiot must be allowed to do some painting.' The awful thing about my tracing these nuts and bolts was that on paper it satisfied The Ministry of Works.

It was all a farce, a tragic comedy which went on for three years and helped to send me completely off my rocker.*

Head lithograph

---

*Albert suffers a severe nervous breakdown and is discharged from 'The Plant' on March 18th, 1944.

Herbert Houthuesen c.1943   The RAF Museum, Hendon

When I was ill and away from the Plant, my cousin, an airman, Herbert Houthuesen*
called on us, literally out of the blue. I hadn't seen him since we were children – the
usual idiocies with our family. I started this portrait but I was so tied up with being
a tracer that it was very difficult for me to sit down and suddenly start painting.

Herbert Houthuesen

Albert was particularly struck by the helmet and the goggles. He thought this had a
medieval air of helmetry about it. I can't remember which of my relatives had told me
about Albert, but I'd heard a great deal about him; and in Africa I'd thought a great deal
about him. I had a tremendous admiration for the fact that he was an exceptional, hard-
working chap. He was the only one I could look up to in my family, as having any real
power of application. I thought he was a magnificent sort of father-figure amongst
our rather fatherless relatives and I did want to meet him very much.

It wasn't until the war that I got in touch with him and he made one feel very welcome.
He knew a great deal about almost any place I mentioned. What happened there,
its artistic background, how they lived and a cunning knowledge of the way
they operated. I suppose all my life, having had a fairly stormy one, I've searched
for something which is orderly, forceful and well-directed.

*The son of one of Albert's mother's step-brothers.

127

Somnambulist 1943-1966 watercolour

When Cath and I moved to Tickhill, we met a carpenter called William Green –
a remarkable character. He was a highly nervous man who really wanted to be a painter.
Various things in his life had stopped this so that just the very idea that I tried to draw
and paint drew us together. William would come home latish in the day, wash, have his
tea, and sit down for a few minutes. And then, until daylight went, he would work like
a maniac in his garden or shed.

William was the only one who sometimes came into our cottage and saw what it was
like. But there were a lot of people, for instance, who thought I was away from the Plant
because it was more amusing to be away. One day William gave me some roses and I
began to paint *Somnambulist* and *Anvil*. They didn't take twenty-three years. You have
the things by you and you pick them up and pick them up. Everybody else goes mad.
And there you are still working on the same watercolour.

Anvil 1943-66 watercolour and collage

One night, German bombers went over dropping chandelier flares. I looked back – the sound of the bombers seemed to come from behind, in fact it's a funny echo – and then I turned round and the night was absolutely blue with two great chandelier flares hanging in the sky; and the whole village, every tiny speck of it – if a cat had walked across you would have seen it lit up – everything, as if it were carved out of a phosphorescent chalk. I've never seen anything like it. It was like another world.

All the time, wherever one is, one gets a great many things. For instance meeting William Green and the odd people there. One could tell some very funny stories; and there were many situations that happened. Out of Tickhill, I got the walk from Letwell to Langold Pit where I used to get the bus for work. Well, the landscape with the coal-tips was very wonderful to see. In fact, one's painting-life has really been like travelling through some vast landscapes; and the moment one wall has been surmounted and one has gone on a little, then the next wall is there. But I imagine, in any case, that everyone's life is like that – up to a point. There are only very few happy, reasonably well-off men and women who are able to do what they want. The whole of life is one long, long, long struggle.

Farmer Bramley's Prize Gelding* 1944

What so amused me about this horse was that there was a groom holding this animal; and whilst I stood at my easel and worked and the groom was there, this horse stood still. Then I would say to this man, 'Well that's enough for today.' I had to move the easel so that the horse and groom could leave. And as I picked up my easel and the groom moved, this horse would turn around and whisk this fellow out of the stable. This thing literally charged out and it was no joke. It was a staggering, wonderful animal. The painting itself is much too tight. One of the reasons why my paintings and drawings at this time had to be done in this meticulous sort of way was because – and it's an awfully boring thing to have to repeat again and again – they were literally done from one bout of migraine to another. I would be ill for a week from the Plant; and apart from Saturday afternoons and Sundays that was when I would add a section. I hadn't the physique to stand up and brush the whole thing in.

Mr Cook Vicar of Tickhill 1968

I didn't know Mr Houthuesen well but he was a very interesting man and we remember him with affection. He was enthralled by and devoted to his work. It meant everything to him.

Farmer Bramley's Prize Gelding

*Albert wanted to include the groom in the picture, but Farmer Bramley would not agree to this. Before each session, the horse was wiped down with a light paraffin solution to bring out the colour of its coat. What greatly impressed Farmer Bramley was the fact that when Albert painted the horse, it was unshod. The shoes were placed on the ground afterwards and then added.

The Grand

Three Clown Heads 1944 ink

It was a terrible thing to see the planes going over, to think of the marvellous young men on those bombing raids and know perfectly well that many of them wouldn't come back. And that it was going to be ghastly at the other end. One day I thought 'I'm always clowning for friends, trying to cover things up, so I'll give up clowning and start being a clown through some drawings.'

The first clown act I saw as a youngster was of a girl in tights, all very 'piquant and shishi,' handing a juggler a pile of plates. To a roll of drums, he began juggling with them. One, two, three, four, five, six, seven. They went higher and higher, whirling like mad, and he was this 'Jacob's Ladder'. For one moment, he looked up thoroughly alarmed and the whole thing crashed, smashing all these plates. It left me aghast at the thought of all the expense.

Michel Herman 1944 The Theatre Museum

These sketches at the Doncaster Theatre were the first real clown studies I did.
The Hermans were a family of Russian Jews who were all musical clowns. I used to
go round at the back and tell them how marvellous I thought they were. They couldn't
quite understand this because nobody else bothered. People rolled in, laughed like hell
and went out.

Danny Polo 1944 ink   The Theatre Museum

Do you get the idea of this terribly pathetic fellow? He was in fact pathetic and very
poor. His wife for instance took in the washing of the company to help keep them going.

Charles Cameron 1945 ink   The Theatre Museum

When I was away from the Plant, I drew these chaps who were at once rather touching and, at the same time, also had, as this type of clown does have, something rather ridiculous. I suppose in relation to being at the Plant the whole situation was such. It was at once extraordinary and appalling and wonderful and everything else.

I saw Charles Cameron at the theatre. And I was terribly amused because he could pull these extraordinary faces by simply taking his false teeth out. Then finally, at the curtain call, he would look wonderfully normal and polite by putting his false teeth in again. One exaggerates this nonsense with his fingers and makes a design out of it with his fingers moving like the fins of a fish.

21 St Marys Gate
Tickhill
Doncaster
Jan 23rd 1944

My Dear John and Elizabeth,

Thank you <u>very</u> much for "The Poet's Corner" it's a delightful volume, and if I may say so, your introduction is beautifully written. Altogether the book has a double interest for me. Long ago (oh how long ago now!) walking through the Tate I saw Max's "Rossetti and his Circle". How I enjoyed them, and how remarkable I thought them. I was not yet at College then, but I knew everyone of the characters, and one simply said to oneself "That's it!" I felt I knew them exactly in just that way, and it seems to me that *one cannot praise an artist's work more than that. Fordy Brown frowning whilst being patronised, and Gabriel's courtship, a beauty!*

Later your father showed me the portrait reproduced though I met Max earlier. One evening at 13 A.G. a young author talked gaily away and ended by saying "What with this trend and what with that trend a young man today doesn't know what to be!" Max, with that slow, hesitant speech which made one listen to every word, said, witheringly, "what's…….. wrong……..with……..just being yourself?"

The way it was said was so crushing that the young man said goodnight and departed.

Out of the blue came a letter from Sir Walter Lamb (Jan 21ˢᵗ) asking me for the date of my birth with reference to my nomination for A.R.A. It seems they are looking for a president!

Adieu my dear ones,

A very happy new year from us both.

Albert

Danny Polo 1945 ink   The Theatre Museum

Ruisdael's Redoubt
Sept 24ᵗʰ 1944

Dear John,

Thank you for your letter and form. I hope this will be sufficient? Fame crowds upon me so fast where shall I stop? Nottingham has just purchased a still life (36 x 28) and since I was discharged from the L.N.E.R office I am busy with commissions. And the importance of being born in 265 Albert Cuyp Straat!

Adieu, and Greetings
from
Albert

Prisoner's Garland 1940-46 inscribed on the stretcher: AHT
Bough and Garland from a lost orchard, Garland from a vale of shadows by 769 LNER Doncaster

I had started this crock before 1940, when I had thought of painting a whole series of
smashed up jars I had collected. Through my being ill, this broken crock was seen as a dead
thing carrying these branches that looked literally dead and yet were flowering. And this
main idea of something that has just come down or been torn away came to me at the Plant.

What is so strange to me now is seeing this black and white photograph held like that.
It's just like the sky, a dark sky with light clouds, dark rock and the sea and foam.
It could absolutely be the foam dashing against the rock and travelling across it.
It's inevitable that there are these similarities since these things are painted because
they are oneself. You see this branch which, in spite of everything, somehow tries
to flower, is me carrying my troubles whatever they are.

There is a very curious story which has just come to me. Shortly after the war, I thought I would send this picture to the Royal Academy, but it was rejected. When I had collected the picture, I leaned it against the wall – I have always had a feeling for the oddness of the life of a picture. To see a thing that one has made and worked over – it's really a very private thing – standing on the pavement, was like seeing some beautiful piece of china that had been knocked over.

At that moment, a little girl of about ten with a small brother and her little sister of about six, wonderful Cockney kids, came by and they stopped dead in front of the picture. The smallest child walked forward, pressed her grubby fingernail on it – I saw the canvas go in – and said 'That belongs to Jesus.' The older girl said 'Shhh' and hurried her away. There is something innocent, I would say, in the picture and there was some innocence in the child that perhaps linked it with putting flowers round a plaster statuette or something like that. Anyway I was delighted with the little girl for saying such a wise thing.

One would like to be able to explain and talk about these things simply but in fact the reason why something like that came about is quite complicated. There I was at the Plant, loathing the very idea of war, this ghastly lunacy, yet having to do this idiotic work. And I had been thinking a great deal about Saint Bernadette.* She did have a vision whatever one may think. A little while before, I had seen this extraordinary little photograph of her which I had pinned up in my minute workroom in Tickhill. And it is possible that something of the thoughts of this mystery gets into one's work and into one's being. What I mean is I've never had something like that said by a child or anyone else over anything. But I did over this.

Laura lithograph

*In 1858, Bernadette Soubirous, an asthmatic girl of fourteen, was collecting firewood on the edge of Lourdes for her homeless family. Beside the grotto where she stood flowed a stream. It was there that the Virgin Mary first appeared to her in a vision. And told her to drink from the waters. Bernadette tasted only mud but a spring of cold, crystal-clear water bubbled up. Pilgrims began to flock to Lourdes as news spread of the grotto's healing waters. St Bernadette entered a convent and died in 1879.

Return to London

Italian Peaches 1947

Very soon after the war was over, we came to London. The students of Kate's College were billeted out to various places and since we had lost our home, we were asked to be wardens at the Lady Margaret Vicarage in Chatham Street, close by the Elephant and Castle.
Of course we jumped at this, because it gave us a roof, a west room with a biggish window where I could work and two other rooms – for twenty-five
pounds a year rent.

Can you imagine me being a very stern warden and having to look after twelve beautiful girls? It was quite a strain in some ways. We were supposed to 'book in' and 'book out' these girls but fortunately they were all very respectable and well-behaved; and made no disasters over anything. One also had to lock up the place at night and attend to fatuous telephone calls. But it was paradise – the moment the war was over and the killing had stopped. I can't describe to you the incredible feeling of no longer hearing the bombing planes going over. That's still the most appalling sound to me. At night if I hear these planes going over, I always think of the bombers.

Another Princess lithograph

137

Near Borough High Street c.1946 ink wash   AHT

Being back in London was in itself wonderful. I wandered round literally through sheer nostalgia. I walked and walked and walked – everywhere. The East Street Market in Walworth was one ruined shop after another; and people simply improvised boxes and planks as counters for selling their wares. There would be some little unclaimed ruin and some amazing chap selling shoe-polish and laces. In the corner would be a trunk lying upside-down and cushions left from a fallen ceiling; then a burnt-out staircase all-to-view.

It was incredible scenery – the vitality of it all, the improvisations of people going on with the work of the day in these ruins. There were all sorts of people who came and went, just as it is when one walks along the street and you rub shoulders with everybody. I think that at this time one did become a little freer. But for all that is worth, I would have become freer without the disaster. One can't, in a way, separate any of these things. They are all inextricably linked.

Undertones of War 1945-6 charcoal   AHT

One day some very amusing cockney children came into my workroom; and one small girl pointed to a black pastel drawing of melons, apples and pomegranates, and said 'That's war'. She saw fighting in this still-life. I was absolutely amazed because to me that was the truth about these things. With these children, the mind is unmodelled and the reaction is absolutely direct and, I like to think, true. I haven't made drawings of soldiers fighting, or whatever it may be in relation to war, but all this comes into one's work. Everything you've been thinking about must.

Pomegranates 1946

We bought fruit from a marvellous Italian cockney greengrocer who worked round the corner. One day he was passing the workroom window, this western window through which the sun poured. There was no curtain and he could see my easel, so I felt I must show him the picture. There was a tremendous business of miming; and he was saying 'Ah, very good, very good' and we got to know each other. I bought fruit which was unripe and tough. He understood absolutely what one wanted.

I'm always amazed when I pass the greengrocer's and see these boxes in which the fruit is kept apart with pieces of purple or violet or light pink tissue paper. Seeing grapes and pears and peaches wrapped in these papers, reflecting the colour and light is, in itself, a most beautiful sight. It links up with other things.

To me, these peaches with their tissue paper are just like a great shore with the sea and surf; and every peach a sun. One paints it over and over again.

Ana Nevada

Inside cover of the May 1946 'Adelphi Sketchbook' containing the drawings reproduced below (The Theatre Museum).

I was avid to go to the theatre. The two ballet companies which really interested me were Covent Garden and the Ballet of the Champs-Elysées at the Adelphi. At that time I went more to the Adelphi. It was small and more intimate; and the company was small and very exciting. The ballets were various, very charming and full of life. They all fell under certain headings – they have to, like paintings. They were about falling in love or being rejected or dying or a festival. For me, they gave a general impression of what life is about with the rather Spanish accent governing the idea.

There was a dancer called Juanito Garcia, a dwarf figure, who hammered it out with tremendous power. And there was Ana Nevada. She was a remarkable looking girl and a beautiful dancer. In this particular thing *Los Caprichos* I have never heard castanets speak as she made them speak. She was far and away the best of that company.

I made a little notebook and gradually the drawings came. Sometimes I arrived home and made a few scribbles but often I would be much too excited. And in a way, one has to be quite detached and calm. I tried to draw in this notebook in the theatre, while these things were going on and do what amounted to 'shut eye' drawings. You can't, as a penniless nobody, ask good dancers to stand for you for some hours, so you do it from memory. I went backstage – they were all there – and I made notes; and in one way it suited me better. Nevada's mama thought that I was interested in her daughter and she couldn't believe that I really wanted to watch this dancer at her work.

I remember saying to Nevada
'Let me see how you hold the castanets
with those index fingers straight as a die.'
I watched that many times.

Also inscribed by Ana Nevada, with her address

For viewing the ballet as an entirety, the stalls are hopeless. For a painter, it's very interesting because you get the tremendous immediacy of the living figures; but for the illusion – the whole thing in its entirety – you should sit way back in the Dress Circle.

You can't make drawings of a racehorse tearing round a track on the spot. At least I can't. I look many times and remember something of it. Finally you have to work from memory and try and absorb what you can. It's a curious thing but after a time, the memory begins to be even stronger. If I think about it now, those particular ballets are very vivid to me.

Sometimes I thought 'I must remind myself to take photographs.' Of course there were these illustrated books at the theatre; but oddly enough, I've never been able to draw or paint from them. For Degas, the camera was a very intriguing and rather wonderful thing, which it is; and I think Degas used it wonderfully. But he had this calmness which I haven't got. If I think of a ballet that I've seen and then look at a photograph of Antonio posed in that particular ballet, the photograph to me is a completely dead thing.

One sees these things and has such a memory of them that it sometimes isn't necessary to leave the house. Also the moment I begin to work, the memories flood back even more strongly. To produce work makes one go on. It's as if it generates something else in one and awakens it all again.

I happened sometimes to use a black ink medium because for me it was an expressive one and I suppose, if one stops to think about it, with the Spaniards, although there is a great deal of richness of colour, there is also great blackness. Again and again with these particular Spanish ballets – the girl and the 'Duena' and so on – there are figures in black. The Spaniards are terribly serious. It's a life and death struggle. And many of these ballets are just that. The Spaniards are like that themselves, terrific realists like the Hollanders. So perhaps there is something in it that I understood. Some chord.

The little Spanish Ballet had this deep traditional idea rather than some lightweight amusing thing which filled in ten minutes. And since the artists were good – and I must underline that because it wouldn't otherwise have come home so forcibly – I saw acted things that I had myself experienced in a very different way. It was really my Mama and it came home again and again, so terribly and incredibly. For Cath and for me, it was the story of how our marriage was too much for Mama. You either survived or you were wrecked. That's why I made these little notes and why they mean so much to me.

The mother's over-guarding of her daughter, and her inability to see that anyone could want simply to congratulate her daughter on her beautiful dancing – that she couldn't get around that point and was herself such an incredible 'Duena' – was so unbelievably real. I think it was what wrecked that girl's career and why one never heard of her again; because she was never alone. And an artist must stand on his or her own feet; otherwise it's like having a millstone around one's neck.

Not in sketchbook 1946

Los Caprichos (The Caprices) was inspired by the Goya etchings of the same title. The ballet depicts a young 'Majita' pursued by a succession of suitors who attempt to seduce her. Indifferent to each, she falls in love with a toreador. But he abandons her, leaving her prey to regrets and nightmares.

Duena and Dancer 1947 pencil   AHT

It's grotesque but it's me and what I wanted to do.

Duena 1947 ink and gouache   AHT

Duena and Dancer 1947 ink

Castinets c.1949

'Something new to London in dance recitals, though common enough in Paris, was presented yesterday afternoon by a small French company 'Les Etoiles de la Danse.' It was less chilly than the ordinary dance recital because relays of dancers made it possible to eliminate the frequent waits between short items that are fatal to solo recitals....Best of all, however, were the solo Spanish dances of Mlle Ana Nevada. 'Cordoba', 'Rhapsodie Valencienne'. The 'Ritual Fire Dance', and a Bolero, in which classical technique with points and half-points was mingled with Spanish steps, displayed the brilliance, vivid personality, and technical range of a dancer whose like has not been seen here since La Argentina died.'

Times Tuesday January 6th 1948.

Ana Nevada and Juanito Garcia

Nevada was a beautiful creature to watch – a sheer delight. She always brought the house down. In *Los Caprichos* she did this fire dance beautifully and I simply marvelled that having made such an impression and been so remarkable, she goes out just like a candle. And nobody notices that she's gone.

Ana Nevada 1950

I've seen some very remarkable ballets and I've been moved to tears through steps that I've watched because they have, for me, so vividly portrayed the emotions which one has experienced oneself. That's why these dances have come about. They're based on fact.

At the time, one only thinks of the dancer and the movement. Afterwards it may look like a wave of water going over a rock. But at the time, one doesn't have that complicated sort of thinking.

Certain things stand out for me, like *Petrushka* and *Le Tricorne*. And *Les Sylphides* was one of the most beautiful things I've ever seen. Alas, I missed seeing Nijinsky, but seeing photographs of him, made up as this puppet symbol under this tremendous magical power, is deeply moving.

Massine was the most remarkable male dancer I ever saw. He came to direct the English Company in *Le Tricorne*. They did it marvellously. Massine was given a tremendous ovation and certainly I have never seen the Company do *Le Tricorne* like that.

Tricorne lithograph

Massine in *Le Tricorne*

I was so moved by Massine's rendering of 'The Miller' that I thought, 'Well, I've never seen this man close-to, so I'll wait.' I went round to the stage entrance and I waited. A Rolls-Royce limousine drew up and I thought 'He won't be long now.'

It was such a funny picture. All the fans having by now gone, the streets at night looking so beautiful, and here I was standing by this limousine. Suddenly Massine appeared and after him, his wife and a young male dancer. But Massine led the way. I was so amazed at seeing this very handsome, startlingly small man that the only thing I could do was to absolutely fix him, devour him with my eyes – the rudest thing one could do. He may have thought 'Well isn't this ass going to say something?' But I couldn't – this terrible thing happens to me, it goes right back to other things.

Still we looked at each other for an unconscionable time. In the meantime the chauffeur had opened the car door. Massine bowed to his wife and she stepped in; then he beckoned to the young dancer to go into the car; and then he stepped in. The chauffeur closed the door and off they went.

Clown Conjurer c.1949

You go to the theatre and see some nonsense review and there is always something wonderful. Two or three people in such and such a costume, wearing hats and tap dancing. I love to hear good tap-dancers telling their rhythmical story – the ballet of the day. Their shoes are like castanets. They would either come on with these amazing clown costumes, or immaculately dressed, and move across the stage tap-dancing all the way.

They all have their genius to me. I can't stand it when it's pretentious, sentimental rubbish as one can see on the telly any night. To me, it's an absolute tragedy the rubbish that is performed.

These people all have their own character and beauty. How I loved seeing them, each one earning his living in this extraordinary way. When you think of it, the theatre is sheer entertainment, though it can be terribly serious for all these people who, like artists, are leading very precarious lives. It's amazing to think of the backbreaking work of a ballet dancer just to be able to perform a few steps with precision and real elegance. Yet people give their lives for these things. Sometimes I've seen people who are quite unknown and they have been terribly funny at the time. And then they disappear like autumn leaves. When you see a Marcel Marceau, there's no forgetting him. That's the difference.

Tiny Hat lithograph

150

Over the years, I've seen marvellous puppet figures and heads. They're frequently grotesque exaggerations; and if they're good, each one has a tremendous vitality. But these puppets are a synthesis of certain characters. I've seen Sicilian puppets – the beautiful 'Virgin Maid,' 'The Crusading Knight' and 'The Moor.' They're wonderful. Everybody knows the story, just as everybody knows the Punch and Judy show, and is able to join in. You can see it a hundred times. I often think that Rouault was, in a profound way, inspired by these very vital images. They have an abstraction; and I adore things that have what is, to me, this strangeness.

The other evening, on telly, we heard a Jamaican steel band. The tragedy was they were playing modern operas, something like *Madame Butterfly* instead of doing what those drums and only those drums could give. But the mimicry of it was extraordinary – just by ear of course – because no man could read music.

I remember being carried away when the Balinese and Javanese people came to London with their marvellous Gamelan orchestras. I went as often as I could to see them. Until now, it is the oriental richness of it which fascinates me. I can't imagine anything more marvellous than those girls with their incredible head-dresses, absolutely encased and standing like columns of gold. One could say that my not having drawn and painted them simply means that they don't interest me. I think it's because I don't understand it enough yet. Maybe one day I'll be able to do something about it, but it won't be through knowing about the detail of the costumes. It will be the idea of it.

Melons 1945

The theatre is always in my head, just as the desire to paint is always there. At this time, I was also painting still-lives. I'm not very conscious of dates or figures, but afterwards, I look back and see that perhaps I did half-a-dozen melon pictures. I loved the richness and the strangeness of these melons; and I was delighted when I found out that, because of their great brown blotches, they were called 'Tiger Melons'.
They are my 'Tyger, Tyger burning bright, in the forest of the night.'

Cedar Tree 1952   AHT

Oxted

Gradually things became more normal and the vicarage became a vicarage again.
The girls went to larger hostels nearer to the College. And Kate and I had to find
another place to live. Through a friend, we went to Stone Hall in Oxted. It was a
staggering, derelict, creaking ruin with over forty rooms. The ceilings were falling in
and none of the doors would lock. It had been a lovely house and originally the garden
had been famous for its beauty. We understood that the place was to be rebuilt, but
nothing of a sort happened. It was one long disaster which had hilarious sides to it.
The thing that I loved there was once again having the seasons, the beauty of the
countryside, the marvellous trees, the space and the great scenery.

There was a huge and magnificent cedar tree from which storms blew off branches the
size of trees. This tree was highly dangerous and we used to risk our lives picnicking
under it. One night there was a tremendous storm and half the tree was burned down.
A big billiard room became my studio. And from the window, I could look out onto this
broad, overgrown lawn covered with such long grass that it was like a miniature field.

Roses 1952

The garden was huge and studded with rhododendrons and rose bushes and little sapling trees which grew at an amazing speed, interspersed with great and very old magnolia trees. Underneath arches of weeds, you would come upon a patch of crocuses in bloom, looking as though someone had dropped a casket of jewels. There were huge ant-heaps. I touched one with my foot and I've never seen anything like the hive of activity of these creatures.

One day I was walking along a fence which had been part of someone's chicken run; and suddenly I saw a fully-grown male fox run towards this fence – he saw no way out – and try to jump it. It hurled itself against the wire and was thrown back. It saw that I was standing still and tried again. And again it was thrown back. It made several attempts and then it turned away from me and ran under a long, tall hedge.

Vision of St Eustace c.1950

Daffodils and Magnolia in Enamel Jug 1952

It was all a staggering wilderness of chaos. We lived in one downstairs room and an upstairs room which we used as a bedroom. People were circulating around us all the time and it was quite a mad existence; and not exactly conducive to concentrated thought. One longed for peace and quiet. And in July 1952, we moved to this house. It was the first time in our lives that we had had a roof which eventually became our own; and where we could live without other people in the house.

Love Walk

Wrestler Charlie lithograph

It is an absolute fact that not until we were in this house was I able to come to terms with the terrible reality of my father's death. And one afternoon I began to tell Kate about it, for the first time. Here was the first real peace we had known. And if one can give a reason for the seascapes then it is probably because of this.

I cannot tell you what a paradise it is for us to be here, in this quiet place with a roof over our heads, knowing that we are not going to be chucked out. I look at the sky and the vast clouds became a seascape. I put my colours out and the moment I have annihilated this frightening white of the canvas, I'm lost in it again. I struggle through the surf and I'm battered against the rocks. And there it is.

Sea Shell lithograph

Rocks, Sea and Sky 1956-57

I do think that if later on my pictures began to have more movement, it was through watching dancers. The more I was able to go to the ballet, the more moved I was by it. And the more I came to realise that the clouds, the sea, poetry and the movement of the dancers were all the same thing.

5 Love Walk
Denmark Hill. S.E.5
April 6th 1954

Dear Elizabeth and John,

I just wanted to thank you for your effort on my behalf to the Leicester Gallery. It was very kind of you, one of these days the introduction will, I hope, lead to something good. These things take time, and certainly no one is slower than I am.

But I do thank you for all the trouble you had and went to for me. I hope it won't be too long before we may meet again.

Ever Yours,
Albert

Dear Elizabeth and John,

I just wanted to tell you that Mr Roland and his wife called last Friday evening. They could not stay long, but, briefly, my work for Mr Roland is "too finished." He did however say that he would speak to the O'Hana Gallery about me, but I asked him not to do so, at least for the time being. I hope you will understand what I mean. I have no intention of working in a particular way for a particular gallery. The little I have gained has been through much hard toil, and trying always to complete a work to the utmost, as well as I can.

Once again I do sincerely thank you for your interest on my behalf, if it should happen one day that I had a little success it would please me very much, and I believe it would give pleasure to my friends.

Ever Yours,

Albert

P.S.

I do hope that Roland's disapproval will not disturb you. Sometimes in the past I have allowed my anger to run away with me, afterwards I have always deeply regretted it, one must accept these things, make no reply and persevere. We all have worries enough, and I should hate to think that these criticisms might in the slightest way upset you.

Sentinel Rocks 1963

Rocks and Spray 1961

Mama began to give us hell here. She came to stay with us for three months. And this terrible scene happened one afternoon. I couldn't have done this particular thing early in the morning. Mama had her back to me and at that moment, during her tirade, I nodded with my eyes to Kate who was receiving the worst of it. I picked up an ordinary white plate and threw it down with a crash. And the plate didn't break. Mama turned round astonished. I then smashed the plate with my foot and said 'Now will you stop it, Mama. We can't go on like this.' And Mama looked at me with great dignity, walked to the cupboard, took a broom and very quietly began sweeping. The tables were completely turned. Mama knew she had always pushed one as far as she could go or thought she could go. This was the first time that I had ever replied to her. The first time. And the Lord defended the plate.*

*After this incident, Catherine takes Albert's mother to her own flat in Hampstead. She is in fine spirits whilst Albert is ill in bed for a month.

When I was by the sea, I just looked at the sand and the water, the rocks, the horizon, the skies. I certainly didn't start thinking about its significance and my mother. These things are very profound. And afterwards, with what one has seen and experienced in life, they may well be true. When I pick up a small canvas and begin painting the sea, I see the movement of it – the going out and the coming back – it's erotic. And I see the sky with veils of rain moving across. And I hear the water. It comes as quite a shock when the boy arrives with the groceries. It is difficult to analyse why one is moved by something. It's as if an idea grips you by the scruff of the neck and you just have to go on with it. There's no such thing as inspiration as far as I'm concerned. Only hard work. A man like Constable was absolutely gripped by the trees against the sky. He was born

Stonemason lithograph

to that, and it was inevitable that he should make these marvellous landscapes.

The moment one says 'Gainsborough' 'Rubens' or 'George Stubbs' you have the man and what he is involved with. To me, Gainsborough is so staggering. His nature is lyrical but very powerful. People are deluded. He gives the essence and quality of absolute grace but really he is a tough fellow. He has the dance in him and his figures float.

Peaches and Mulberry Leaves (with Angel in bottom left corner) c.1955

It is the character of a man that makes him work at it all day and dream about it at night to a degree that another, who is not so completely absorbed, does not.

Vincent was completely absorbed; and Manet, for all that people have said about his being a light, gay and amusing fellow which I'm sure he was, was completely absorbed. That's why he's survived because of his character.

The subject is like a mysterious ghost, a chimera, which disappears. It haunts you. You try to catch it and always you are eluded. I can stand by the fountains in Trafalgar Square and be absolutely renewed by listening to them and looking at them in the mist. Anyway the psychologists and psychiatrists will have a lot to say about my longings and my vast frustrations, the symbol of the sea. And the mist.

Looking Down from a Height c.1955-1959

July 19th 1959

My dear Elizabeth and John,

I felt I must write to you. I want to thank you for calling and for bringing Madame Escarra-Champetier de Ribes and Mr Silbermann. Everyone was so kind and you all gave me such encouragement, that I am filled with hope. I am filled with ideas for work, and somehow, suddenly I have quite a new hope and belief that things will be done, and that it will all bear fruit. At this moment my head is in a whirl, it's an extraordinary feeling of hope you have given me, to say nothing of your real practical help. I am so glad you have the drawing and the seascape. It's as if through this beginning one day the work will be known.

Greetings, my many thanks,
and all good wishes,
Albert

Dancers c.1969

Antonio would dance the 'Zorongo' with two guitars and sometimes a singer. It is a marvellous moment when he holds his hat and encases Rosario. In fact they don't ever touch each other. One evening, I saw them both taking curtain calls together. As they were bowing, this girl touched his cheek, carried away for a moment by the tremendous applause. He was furious and would have nothing to do with it.

The greatest Spanish dancers I ever saw were Antonio and Rosario. They were absolutely marvellous. And it was very melancholy for me to see that Antonio felt he must develop in the 'modern sense' and make it bigger and more elaborate. And in a way lose a great deal of the original purity.* The clothes that Antonio and Rosario wore, with masterpieces of jewellery, were absolutely authentic and very beautiful.

*Antonio's return to London in Spring 1955 was reviewed by Cecil Smith (Daily Express, 22.2.1955):
'Antonio danced with his cousin Rosario until a quarrel ended their partnership in 1952. In a way he is lost without her. He has surrounded himself with a company of inferior dancers who behave more like cabaret entertainers than serious exponents of classic and folk dancing. This is lamentable but Antonio is still so dazzling at 32, so that I could forgive him everything when I watched him.'

Rocks and Storm 1956-58

I first saw the sea as a child in Scheveningen. And in Amsterdam the feel of it was always there. Much later I saw and heard the raging and ravening beasts and dragons that guarded the coast of beloved England with hearts and bones of flint instead of dykes of earth and wood.

The sea has always fascinated and terrified me. If there is anything in the seascapes, then it is because of an attempt to overcome an overwhelming sense of despair. I see the hardship and suffering of human beings in the eternal wrestle of sea, rocks, and land. And I paint the sea again and again eating the world away.

People say so and so was a seascape or a landscape painter. But if you can draw and paint one thing, you can draw and paint everything. Things are going through one's head all the time. And obviously one sometimes has a melancholy mood; or a more gay mood or a spring mood. I find that the weather and the day have an effect on me. I look at the sky and I hear the sea.

I go for a walk and see two or three motor cars abandoned in the street, completely battered with re-enforced glass, like sparkling dust, about the pavements. It looks so incredible and I wish I could make some comment. Yet it is through not underlining these things that I have tried, in an oblique way, to say something about them.

Rocks and Sea, Great Orme, N.Wales c.1963

AHT

Young Ancestor lithograph

This is as I imagined a junk to be which is wrecked on these rocks. It took three weeks to paint and I call it *Wreck of the Early Hope*. It is in relation to my struggle and finally getting here. As a child, these boats attracted me. I must have seen them on small coloured Japanese prints that Father had. It only struck me the other day that this picture and the *Icarus* may also have come about through these great red lacquer screens and chests which I first saw at Fry's and loved.

June 10th 60

This morning the "Early Hope" and the "Gateway" went to the Reids in Cord V. The first things of mine ever to go to a picture Dealer, knowing that they will be accepted.

Shipwreck* 1935 pencil

*Albert felt this shipwrecked vessel he saw and drew in 1935, had a subconscious but direct bearing on *Wreck of the Early Hope*. The ship had run aground on treacherous rocks in Hope Cove, Salcombe, Devon.

Wreck of The Early Hope March 1960

I think these junks are so beautiful. And I have always thought of them as being something very ancient, very primitive and very frail – ready to be smashed on any rock and every ill that life holds. Yet I have the feeling that they are as eternal as an autumn leaf which curls up and becomes like a thin brown sea-shell and remains so for years and years. I marvel at the journeys these incredibly frail-looking boats make. When men have been such fools as possibly to knock this world to pieces so that there may not even be the metal boats we have, then – if people survive – these wooden boats will come again. To me, they are at once fragile and eternal.

As a study this junk would be very wrong. It is the fragility of this shell-like shape held hard upon these rocks which, to me, is the wreck of my early hope. And I like to think that this light which travels all the way round and gives it this shape, is symbolic of the fact that though one may be a wreck, one has attempted to do something. That in itself is a sacred thing and one's duty.

A Toute à L'Heure 1961-67 Fragments from a still-life laid down on painted board

After an operation I destroyed a number of drawings and paintings. Much later, returning to the workroom, I found everything in it covered thick with dust. As I picked the fragments up, each canvas shape made a clear silhouette upon the worktable. This was made from one canvas. Lying alone in the antechamber, hearing snatches of a conversation in French 'a toute a l'heure' were the last words overheard before losing consciousness.

Written by Albert on the stretcher and dated Aug 3rd 1967

The nurse had said to me with such alarm, 'Pourquoi à toute à l'heure, cherie?' And this picture came about very much through that particular experience and the odd over-hearing of this flirtatious conversation between the girl and the anaesthetist. She shouldn't have left me and she came in and said 'Oh, how are you, Mr Houthuesen?' I said 'Pourquoi à toute à l'heure, cherie?' It was only my intention to pull her leg, but she was terribly alarmed so that the conversation itself must have been pretty serious. Perhaps it's just as well that I didn't know. Certainly it wasn't a very amusing moment for me to be alone. It was a terribly hot summer and the anaesthetist, a wonderful looking young man came in, with a tight-fitting white cap, white boots and just a vest and apron – bare arms. We were on the top floor of the Gordon Hospital, and I saw all this against the light of the window with the tower of Westminster Cathedral behind him. The next morning when the same nurse came into the room, I said – not really realising what was going on – 'Aha, à l'heure, à toute à l'heure ma cherie.'

But for modern surgery, I wouldn't be here now and able
to talk my nonsense, sitting in this warm room with the cat
occupying the armchair. One is eternally grateful to these
dedicated men and women. There are saints among them.

I returned home after my operation,* in a state of despair,
and literally thought I was going to die. I deliberately
destroyed a number of canvasses. The fragments were left
on the table and in the wastepaper-basket. Afterwards, I was
unable to work and didn't go into the studio for a couple of
months. Everything was covered in dust and there had also
been one of these beastly fogs which leaves everything thick
with black smuts of smoke. I began to clear the fragments
off the table; the shapes were all silhouetted and that gave

Armchair Clown lithograph

me the idea to make something of these fragments. I collected pieces from a Melon
canvas painted just after the war, and began to put them together. I envisaged something
like this and marked on the panel where they were to be placed. It began with these
outside strips; and Cath stuck most of these things down because I used to collapse.

A Toute à L'Heure is, I am sorry to say, the largest picture I have yet painted. I enjoy
a largish canvas. I love it. But for me a 25 by 30 inch canvas can be very big. To paint
something that size in a small room like this is quite a strain. You want space and a good
light over the whole thing. The moment you are in a large and uncluttered room and you are
faced by a large area of canvas or board then, at once, you feel you can tackle it. It's purely
a practical question. I always hope that a picture can be knocked on the head as soon as
possible. Strike the iron whilst it's very hot indeed – if you can. Sometimes it happens that
a picture can grip you and become like an octopus – although I never remember thinking
about it – 'I must do this because this isn't strong enough, or because it's too strong.' I can't
tell you how one does it, such as it is. Whether a picture is large or small; and whether it
takes a day or a year, it has, to me, nothing to do with the hoped-for expression. In one way,
the painter should feel that he could go on with every canvas. Sometimes it's just as well he
does. I could go on with this, simplifying and elaborating certain things.

Up to the time we came to this house, I'd never really sold anything. I was getting on and
still I hadn't made a mark of any sort. After the operation, I was very weak. It's rather
dreadful to weep, through sheer weakness, some part of every day for eighteen months.
But I have always had such a desire to draw and paint; and were it not for this, I think
I would have gone long ago. From one point of view, I sincerely hope I don't paint
another *A Toute à l'Heure*. With that canvas, in a small way, I had my say. And if
I were going to say something about it again, it would be said in a different way.

*In April 1961, Albert goes into hospital for a two week check-up. He is released for the private view of his first one-
man exhibition at the Reid Gallery in Cork Street (10th May-3rd June). The exhibition is a success. And Albert returns to
hospital in June for an operation. Six weeks later he is allowed home.

Icarus 1962-67 casein tempera

This *Icarus* panel was begun after I came out of hospital. It is painted in casein tempera.
I'd worked in oil most of the time and one day I looked at casein tempera and painted
some small things with it and loved it. It is Talens from Holland and beautifully ground –
a very rich and lovely medium, as all these mediums are. The marvellous materials one
is offered today. They're like modern medicines.

For me the sun is a symbol of life and hope. The power and beauty of it inspires me
absolutely. Yet to be in it withers me and I have to be in the shade. Like the sea it terrifies
me. Icarus is really the painter. You can see the implication. This constant business of
somehow having to stand on one's feet – the moment one has enough strength – and
go on. And the power of the sun in relation to anything we can manage to do. An idea
grows, and with the 'Icarus', I thought about the eventual destruction of everything;
and this constant desire to build and create which every reasonable human being has.
I hope to paint it again, more richly and more dramatically. But I like this particular,
quiet statement. It isn't a question of the artist being too ambitious. An artist is doomed.
Nothing comes to what he wishes it to be. It's only a shadow of what he hopes for.

The legend is a most marvellous one. People have had these notions for thousands
of years. These ideas have survived because of their profundity. With the roses
I give myself some hope. One must never give up hope.

November 22nd 1963

I made this particular drawing in the morning. And when I turned on the radio that evening, I was astounded to hear that this poor fellow* had been assassinated. I think that this odd sort of coincidence happens because today, with the terrible things that are going on in the world, one's mind is filled with sadness and unhappiness.

Jan 25th 1964

My Dear Elizabeth,

Thank you very much for the colour reproductions. I had seen others but missed those. They are all remarkable, and I know that only good can come of this Pilgrimage. My head is full of Goya, the impact is terrific, and from the R.A. I went to the British Museum. I never quite realised the extent of Goya's profound debt to Rembrandt, they would have embraced each other and wept. At the farther end of the gallery are marvellous things, a Kaigetsudo drawing which I had not seen, and simply <u>beautiful</u> drawings, (3) by Hokusai which I knew but which always strike me in a different way. <u>Remarkable</u>, they are so acutely observed and so true, and two Indian carvings (stone) of dancers, one a drummer, they are at once huge in form and so delicate, and full of movement. The breadth of feeling and understanding of these marvellous sculptors and painters!

*President Kennedy.

26th.

Yesterday Charles Acheson came to tea and stayed to dinner, he is 21 and a fine painter. I hear myself of long ago and today as he speaks. Pearls of wisdom drop from my lips, you should hear our laughter.

11 o'clock.

This afternoon I went again to the Goya, it's no good, I'm as mad about these things now as I was when I was 21, only madder. Many of the Goya's are in a disgraceful condition, how can they? How can the people in authority be so hopelessly stupid?

27ᵗʰ. I must post this now otherwise interruptions will again step in!

> *Goodnight Elizabeth*
> *Goodnight John!*
> *Love from us both*
> *Albert*

Invocation August 1965 Inscribed on the reverse:
The priest Nichiren (1222-1282) stilling a storm at sea by casting a Buddhist invocation upon the waves.

A marvellous idea and just like the story of Christ on the Sea of Galilee. Human beings are human beings. And the thing that fascinated me was the similarity of the legend. And the idea that these profound roots are the same the world over.

Of the Company of St Philemon lithograph

Feb 18th 1965

My Dear John and Elizabeth,

Thank you very much for your letter Elizabeth, and I only hope that your flu and that John's pains have at least eased off, and that life is a bit more reasonable for you both.   I was rushed off to Kings after an unpleasant day, and was there a little over three weeks. It's extraordinary how when I consider the great kindness of everyone concerned, and the confidence I had in the skill of the "Team" under Dr Samuel Oram, how long the time seemed to be. More like thirty years. It's extraordinary to suddenly find yourself part of a great teaching hospital. My voice became the voice of a mouse which was weakness I suppose. One great blessing, thank heavens a thousand times, was the amazing beauty of the nurses. The darlings. What I have I have for ever, but apparently it isn't too serious, it can all happen again, so I hope for the best. I would have answered you before but the pills make me sleep all night and most of the day.

My love to you both
and all good wishes,
Albert

Isn't it odd, I had to come out of hospital for my first ever private view and then go back again. Since Victor Waddington asked me to join him, I wanted with Cath to go to the Jack Yeats private view, but in hospital I had forgotten this and most other things. Late in the afternoon the drs told me I could go home. I tried to phone Cath first at College then at home. No Kate. As I came in by ambulance I had no clothes, so that was that. In the meantime a colleague of Kate's remembered where she was. The first thing the Waddingtons told Cath was that I was waiting to be taken home. But I do wish my life could go along less dramatic lines.

Christ on the Sea of Galilee c.1963

The Bible

I used to like going to church. Most of it I didn't understand but I always had this feeling that there was a great and profound mystery which had tremendous meaning. When you are a child and you read in the Bible of miracles, you wonder very much. Later all that changes and it becomes an amazingly imaginative idea of the world, based on truth, and written by great poets. Man, through this poetry, is trying to express about his life what is so terribly difficult to understand. He stands in mystery and through it he is trying all the time to understand.

Road to Emmaus c.1959

Everything will be revealed one day – we hope. I used to believe the truth was so great that it must prevail. But sometimes I even doubt that. I think that if you live long enough you may then see certain truths revealed.

Still-Life with Fishes and Bread 1961

At certain times, one may begin to make drawings and paintings of biblical things. The Bible is full of these tremendously imaginative ideas. They are profound symbols. The richness of the Bible is terrific. It is the greatest stuff that has ever been written.

I found the Old Testament full of the most terrible things. And I couldn't stand a great deal of the murder and the bloodshed. I thought the New Testament much more humane. As a schoolboy, I would read about the wringing of doves' necks for sacrifice. I couldn't make head or tail of it. It seemed to me unutterably barbaric. I thought some of the stories were tremendous. To choose one is rather like asking which work of Shakespeare is the most remarkable. When you think of Genesis, it's all on a huge Michelangelo-like scale. The force and the character of it are larger than life.

Stage Actors, Adam and Eve lithograph

Jacob's Ladder 1966 casein tempera

When one reads the story of 'Jacob's Ladder' one is moved because this early tale is so profoundly rich and profoundly true of this terribly ambitious man. But is this really just Jacob's Ladder? Isn't it perhaps the end of everything for this chap under this night moon?

Yellow Rose in Glass c.1966

It is a wonderful thing when one is in full swing. The brush in your hand takes over and you don't even know you're painting. It's like praying. Gradually I found that I prayed best when I didn't know I was praying. And I prayed best of all when I was working, because then I didn't even think about praying. Whilst you are drawing and painting, you really are on your knees. It is an adoration of the miracle of Nature and the very fact that you happen to be alive.

Look at these two lilies with these stamens.
What an astounding piece of design this is. How can
you hope ever to get to the bottom of this mystery?
It is that which holds one. It would embarrass me,
in relation to paintings, large or small, to write
'To the greater glory of God.' In a sense, one is
doing this all the time.

If earlier on, I could have been helped to understand
the Bible, how much more quickly one would have
learnt and absorbed certain things. It's a long, long
battle to have to find out everything for oneself.
And in some ways I deeply regret my lack
of education.

Clown with Striped Hat lithograph

September Moon 1971-2 acrylic

Today, for many artists, it's 'out' to be interested in these things. Going to the moon for instance – this incredible thing that has happened in our time – doesn't make the Bible any less wonderful. If anything, it makes it more marvellous. Just as people now say that the romance has gone out of the moon. I saw it the other night, huge over the roofs. Very low, very pale. To me it still looks absolutely astounding. Men have walked on it. But the mystery has remained.

In relation to my ideas as a youngster about the melancholy and solitude of the monks, I really did understand – and I learnt this through seeing pictures of St Jerome, not through literature – why certain men in the past hid themselves away in dark corners with very large, thick books. I thought it was by far the best thing to do. And if I imagined anything like that, then I thought of a largish bare room where somehow I could live painting, almost without eating or drinking. Drawing and painting is a religion if you give your heart and soul to it.

Christ is absolutely real to me. It is his philosophy on how one should behave that has impressed and, I should like to think, influenced me. Most artists are inspired by him. Christ was a great spiritual teacher; about that there is no doubt. And the people who argue against his teaching are like people who are groaning and dying of thirst; and simply won't turn to the jar of water that is to hand.

I am only a very weak man. I can't pray in church today, and in one way that means almost nothing to me. But the fact that these vast buildings – some of them very grand – exist, and that thousands of remarkable men and women have thought along these lines, is a tremendous testament to the thinking of a person. Human beings cannot live without this inspiration. His thinking is an absolute necessity in life; and to me it is as plain as a pike-staff.

Think of the power of not writing a line. Christ just talked to people. The written word is already a second or third-hand thing, but so powerful that this incredible, marvellously humane religion is based on Him. It doesn't come from one man. Christ received it from the synagogues and from the people before him. As a teacher he was a genius. He hits the nail on the head. But in a sense, this is a quality which even supreme artists have. Christ speaks. He didn't do more than speak terrific sense. With Socrates it is the same. He spoke the truth as he saw it.

I think the secret is that some men and women are born with an intense imagination. And this imaginative power gives their thinking great clarity. That is why their thoughts carry on and on and become a universal thing, of all time and for all time.

What can I say about Christ and about Rembrandt? For me they are there all the time. They are both incredible geniuses with this amazing power to express their thoughts. Christ's teachings have lasted for two thousand years; and influenced human beings all over the world. Every man and woman who walks about the street is possibly, even without knowing it, influenced in some way by Christ.

Christ Mocked lithograph

The world of artists, such as it is, is very much smaller. And it is a mere handful who can take what Rembrandt said, through his drawings and paintings, and see that he is a divine painter.

When an artist paints or carves a Christ, he may well have done so because he himself has gone through it. How else can you paint this subject if you don't understand at least some tiny part of it? But this doesn't mean you think yourself a Christ. To me that would be absolutely blasphemous. It wouldn't be to a chap like Durer. He would have told you, 'I am a genius and certainly I'm quite as great as Jesus Christ, so I'll paint a portrait and prove it to you.' Durer was a genius, but there is to me something odd about that state of mind because we do walk in mystery.

As the ages advance, certain things happen in relation to art. For me, the most appalling thing that has happened today is the commercialism of life. And this is linked with a lack of belief. I am absolutely convinced that the people who built the old cathedrals and made the carvings; and painted these staggeringly beautiful things, did have religion. They thought that Paradise would be their reward.

I have a tremendous respect for the genius of the past. If you stand in front of a Memling or a Roger Van der Weyden, you are looking at the work of a saint with the burning desire to make this extraordinary exactitude which is a homage to the truth. I think that most people painting today paint like ruffians invading a football pitch. I don't mean that they have no sensibility or feeling for painting. They have, but it is the very meaning life has for them.

Actor lithograph

It is this lack of belief, the cynicism and the commercialism that make it possible for such absolute junk in music and painting to be talked and written about. It is in an age. But the more one sees of one's age, so the more one is able to go beyond it. A study of grass under a particular light by Constable is timeless. And inevitably so. These people weren't working to a style. Their style comes through tremendous experience because they've hammered away. And eventually it's recognised. But it isn't the self-conscious aping of a method. The marvellous processes of modern reproduction all have their wonderful and terrible side. And what is written about art is often such an incredible muddle. When people write about Titian or Piero della Francesca or Leonardo, they write intelligently; and their studies are based on writings which have already existed for a couple of hundred years. Then you read something on a modern painter by the same author; and frequently it is so disastrous that, to me, it shows how little they know about the old masters – because if this one really understood Piero, he wouldn't write as he does about Jackson Pollock. All these painters have their qualities and try to say quite genuinely what they have to say. But very, very often advocates choose pretty odd favours to bestow upon them.

Still Life with Pear, Cheese and Cup 1963

It all sounds so confoundedly pompous when one puts this into words. But what makes one draw and paint? What makes a Beethoven? There is something very mysterious about being a Delacroix or a Courbet; about being a Manet or a Cezanne; and having this strange, compelling demon which absolutely makes a man go on – it doesn't matter through what. Look at a man like Turner. Seen objectively, it's very remarkable how he went on and worked and developed. It is being inspired. A sort of divine state.

I think it is in the artist; and it is he who recognises it – that's the extraordinary thing. How is it that one person is a Handel or a Mozart out of whom this wonderful music simply pours; and another man hasn't a note of music in him? There is something very special about these people. One knows what is meant when it is said that all men are born equal but they are not. And one doesn't have to be an artist. Many of the humblest people have this quality.

Ordinarily I don't think along these lines. I just say, what a damned good painting this Gauguin is, or what an amazing, happy extrovert chap Rubens was. We all are, I suppose, several people. But I must emphasize that I don't think that Mozart or Handel or Rembrandt went about thinking 'I have something divine in me.' They just got on with the job.

One talks like this when one begins to question. It is all very, very mysterious. And the more one talks about it, the further away one moves from the mystery. What I feel again and again with this idea of evolution in art, is that with something which one would call 'more modern' – for instance a late great Cezanne – it is superficially, startlingly different to a late Hals. But in fact, at the heart of it, Hals and Cezanne are the same. It is this business of the old, old, new. It is another angle of the same thing. People like Cezanne and Vincent studied profoundly and they really did know the old masters. If a painter thinks this is unnecessary for him, he may be right; but it's unlikely that he will be a truly great painter if he doesn't know his Vincent, his Cezanne and much earlier things.

Even if he isn't able to know them through actual experience, there is some profound inner knowledge with which he starts off at birth. It's as if Mozart knows music from the word go. Certainly some people have this quality of understanding far more at fourteen than another has after a lifetime. Eventually, if paintings and drawings have anything at all it is, in one sense, in spite of the art-schools and the galleries.

Today there is this terrible business of everybody having to find 'A way.' But there is no such thing as a way which hasn't been done before. We were talking about Miro. Well you have only to look at certain early Persian and Indian calligraphies to see this. But it is Miro's particular character, his thumbprint which makes it recognisable as his. Many of Klee's things are very much like looking at a Persian rug. Blake was heavily indebted to the engravings of Michelangelo who, in his way, learnt a great deal from the early Greek and Roman sculptures.

Clown with Love Letter lithograph

It is all part and parcel of the same thing. A link in the chain. If you take an amazing fellow like Ruysdael or Constable, Turner or Monet, Stubbs or Cotman, they are all remarkable. Not because one says 'This has not been done before' but because the drawing and painting bears the artist's stamp. It is the man who, once again, is a unique individual. And that is what makes the work remarkable.

A painting or a carving or a piece of music has to stand absolutely alone. There is no doubt about that. When the artist has sometimes written a letter to his brother or his sweetheart about a particular work; and has said 'I went through this and this and what I tried to do was……' well it's another avenue. But finally the thing has to stand on its own. And because of this, it can take a very long time to get through.

Mama's Sunset 1966   AHT

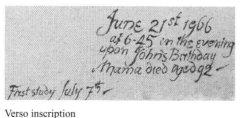

Verso inscription

Bip (Marcel Marceau) as Matador 1975 watercolour

I think that anyone who clowns a great deal is the very one who, in another sense, thinks in a very serious way. It is a comment on despair. And you can see it with a Marcel Marceau or a Buziau. But for this the world would go completely mad.

I've made drawings of clowns and I've only scratched the surface. I would love to paint some large canvasses of these clowns – much richer than anything I've managed to say. One must paint as Marcel Marceau mimes. And I hope I can live to pay, in one's way, a tribute. Marceau is remarkable. People are beginning to criticize him and it's superficial criticism. They think he's done it all before and so on. But that's nonsense. He is trying to perfect what he is doing. And, as far as I'm concerned, he can go on doing these things and making them more perfect and more eloquent. That is what matters.

The critic seems to me to forget, in one sense, that somewhere at this very moment, there is a young man or woman who may one day grow into a great composer. A great musician is somewhere listening to Beethoven or Brahms or Purcell for the first time. And if that hearing or seeing moves them, then it cannot be a dead thing. The other person who has seen certain things and thinks that he has understood them perhaps becomes blasé. And seen from that point of view, the thing is criticised. But I don't feel this about Marceau. I've seen other mimes climbing steps and stepping over walls. But how Marceau does it. That is him. And that's what matters.

Turner becomes more and more enthralled with his theme. Monet ends up by painting his lake, and falls more and more in love with it. And heavens knows how Frans Hals, at the end of his life, did those incredible last pictures. It's really all the same thing. One becomes so involved with something that one no longer thinks about it. One only hopes one can go on.

Johan Buziau

Johan Buziau

I tell you, all the Houthuesens are clowns and they cannot help it. These photographs of Buziau all have such a reality. This is a head with an intense character. It's like a knife. And don't you think the whole idea of being a comedian in professional life is, in itself, altogether fantastic? It's all such a mystery to me and the reason why, in one way, I find it so difficult to talk about drawing and painting. I mean, what is it that makes a man like this take on character after character? His face is literally lined and through the years and years of grease paint, it becomes wrinkled and marked. That's what makes him great. I must give up painting and become a clown. These photographs are incredible.

Johan Buziau (1872 -1958) was the most celebrated comic actor in Holland; and the first cousin of Albert's father (his mother was a Houthuesen). When the Nazis occupied Holland, they placed 'Seyss-Inquart' an Austrian at the head of the Dutch government. Buziau would appear on stage wearing a tiny hat; and say 'Zes en een kwart' ('Six and a quarter' – a play on the Austrian's name) implying 'How could any self-respecting Hollander wear such an absurdly small hat.' It brought the house down. Buziau was placed under house arrest and never performed again. He lived quietly until his death, an ill and nervous man. Our conversation about Buziau took place in July 1968 when Albert saw, for the first time, photographs of Johan Buziau in two out-of-print biographies. Previously he had seen only two or three photographs of his father's cousin.

Look at this commissionaire! The comedy of that hat. It's obviously been designed by him and he absolutely hits the nail on the head. If it's possible to make you laugh, then it comes from this cousin, Johan Buziau. He was a great comic actor. His range was extraordinary.

And this! He's an American tourist abroad. What a fellow! What a fellow! It's wonderfully atrocious. Amazing. I can't take much more of this.

Do you see this? We've all seen musicians making fools of themselves. Look at his idea of a grand-piano. It's just what one feels about it. And he's made it. Isn't it beautiful? It's absolutely living. The whole thing works. I've seen clowns playing about with pianos but I've never seen someone do that design. It's fantastic. Like every good clown he becomes outrageous. The malicious quality in this is simply wonderful. Well thank God he was one of the family is all I can say.

Look at the fantastic characterisation of this cabman!* He's a real London cockney, a Dickensian from what used to be known as the 'Jordaens' in Amsterdam. And I bet he made that horse. What a fellow he must have been. He's absolutely up my street.

*A former champion jockey, he had, with his champion racing horse, been reduced to working as a cabbie in the poorest parts of Amsterdam.

I love that story about the capitalists and the anti-communists. What was it? 'Down with the capitalists. Away with all their possessions, and bring them all to my house.' Looking at this man, can't you hear the deep, expressive Dutch rumbling? One can see he was a perfectionist and a very serious man.

My memories are so vague. Yet I have always had them and these photographs make it a reality. Buziau was already famous. And I remember being taken back-stage and being shown things.

I remember the very smell of the place, the smell of newly-sawn wood and where the wings had been glued together. I remember various people but not a particular person. But the only very clear memory of that visit was of a papier-mâché model of a lying-down baby elephant. I wondered terribly why it didn't move because it was so realistic. Of Johan Buziau's acting, I don't remember a thing. I'm very sorry I couldn't see him.

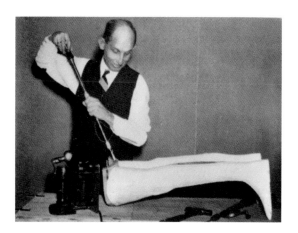

Caption: 'His talent when he plays to a customer who is not there, just that little empty table. His mimicry and the movement of his lips; and all at once his roaring laughter at his customer's supposed joke. The napkin on his arm, his face all white with chalk. He expresses pitiful humility to all the whims of a man who is not there.'

Lately, I've began to think more consciously of Buziau. If only I could have met and drawn him later in life. Till now one has been groping. What an amazing thing it is for me to have these photographs.

Through seeing them, I hope to make a whole lot of things. They give me encouragement in relation to my own clowning and drawing. It's why, in a sense without knowing it, I've done it. Well I can't take any more of them now. I can't.

Self-Portrait or 'Tales My Mother Told Me' 1959 charcoal

If you are taken out of an environment – really taken out of it – then gradually, as you grow up with your brothers and other friends, you clown. Many youngsters do. When I was a kid I did begin to realise certain things and I used to turn the most ghastly situation into absolute comedy. I was eighteen when I managed to talk my mother into my returning to Amsterdam. This situation which I had to pretend didn't really exist, existed so profoundly that I could never speak to my mother about certain things. The truth was avoided and shrouded except that if you keep ears and eyes open and you watch other people, you begin gradually – even if you are an idiot – to understand. Later on, as you grow older and older, you see how things happen in relation to men and women. Then your memory goes back and is consolidated and becomes more and more vivid.

Buziau c.1962

I called these two drawings 'Buziau'
but at the time I had nothing to go on.
These photographs strike a chord.
There is something there but I couldn't
explain it. It's very curious the tricks
one's memory plays. I'm amazed at
how alike these drawings are, but
these things happen.

One can say this of these two drawings –
that I think about my native land every day.
It's there all the time.

Buziau in Top Hat c.1962

I remember these relatives of mine. I remember their laughter. Can you imagine that I don't think about my father and his tremendous clowning, his laugh and finally his cry? All that, if one is anything, is in one's work. I can't tell you how one perhaps puts laughter into a picture. I'm hanged if I know. It's mostly sadness that I remember.

Young White Face lithograph

It is a Houthuesen head. You speak of dungeons and I must say that I have often felt myself to be in one. I'm sure that under the Spaniards, some of my ancestors were quite literally goaled.* But there's the theme and you draw and paint it because it's something you have to say. These things are profoundly in one. I happen to have earned some money and so the next time I go into town, since I have no suit that fits me, I'm going to have something made. And it will be great fun. But other things remain because they are in the blood. When I had those two big music sheets on which the printers had tried out 'Ancestor', what makes me turn one sheet into the Ancestor looking at the Painter Ancestor? I can't put it any other way except that it's something that must be in one's blood. That's what one is. And that's what one's work is.

Jailed Ancestor c.1969 conté crayon, collage

*The hats worn by many of Albert's clowns recall those of his Dutch ancestors - in particular the magnificent Frans Hals standing portrait of Willem van Heythuysen (the artist's only known full length, life-size portrait) and his smaller portrait of Van Heythuysen seated.

Harry Langdon lithograph

This reminds me of Harry Langdon
with this hopeless, all-knowing
innocence. And the feeling that
he's going to get it in the neck.

Johannes lithograph (made after seeing the Buziau photographs).

Flurry of Snow November 1970 acrylic

A Half Worn-Out Brush

When I speak of freedom in painting, I don't mean that a painter can say 'Now, I'm going to take a big brush and smack some marvellous paint on.' That alone is an absolute delight. I can't tell you how many modern, abstract pictures I paint when I start a canvas. I take a white or a red canvas, and I begin with broad masses of colour; and I think to myself, 'God, this is beautiful.' But to me, its beauty only goes to a certain point. By itself, it hasn't enough content. Look at a late Constable, for instance *The Leaping Horse*. It looks as if the paint has been thrown on – just as much thrown on as Jackson Pollock. But compared to Constable, Jackson Pollock, for me, has little meaning or cohesion. I believe Pollock's work is genuine; and this question is all only in relation to the sensibility of a man. Turner was absolutely reckless in those late pictures. But behind that recklessness is a far greater sensibility and concentration.

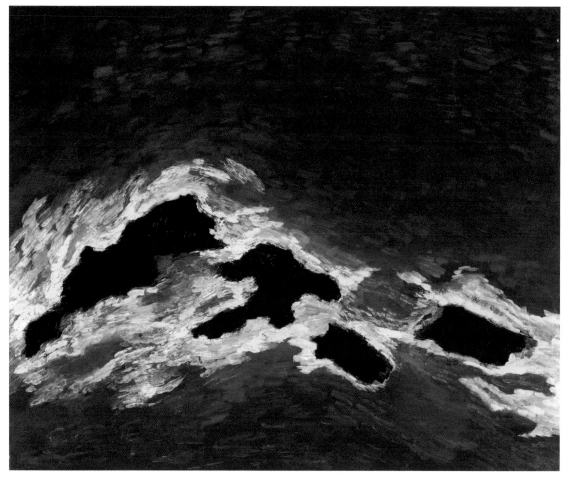

The Leap 1967

To me, Constable's *Leaping Horse* is a miraculous picture. And this means
that he at once knew quite clearly what he was doing; and yet was carried away
by some divine spark about which he could say nothing.

Each picture has its own colour scheme and I like to work within that particular set
of three or four or five colours. I take three or four colours then multiply them and
make my harmony. Every picture, one hopes, lives in its own world, its own mood;
and one doesn't let the moods mix. One makes a painting, not with the number
of colours but with the preparation and preponderance of one colour upon another.
The moment you begin – if you can begin – you have only to take the tubes out of
their covers and put the colours onto the palette; and that in itself is so exciting.
They are so rich. And the disaster is when, with all your longing to paint a rich
picture with these staggering colours, you see them becoming greyer and greyer,
which is oneself.

Always I work with the hope that a picture is going to be painted in an hour. Of course it never comes off and before you know it, you are climbing mountains you'd never envisaged. Before it was going to be a little rocky plain you could walk over easily; and the next minute you're trying to ford rivers which are impossible to ford. During the process of making it an actual thing, I alter it – sometimes tremendously and sometimes wandering so far from what I'd hoped for that the whole thing is just a disaster. And one begins again. But now if somebody doesn't like these things, I shrug my shoulders and I don't put my foot through them. I have destroyed some of these canvas-boards; and one had its revenge on me. There was a tremendous whip-back from this thing and it cut my shin – so don't do it.

Through the centuries, painters have found a light Venetian red or a straw colour to be a wonderfully happy and sympathetic ground on which to work. Certainly it is for me. You can see it in dozens of canvasses that have come down to us. Constable uses it with absolute genius. His main priming is this particular tone of light-red which perhaps has yellow and white added. And that beautiful red comes in through the sky, through the trees and through the houses.

All I have done is stick to very simple and known techniques. I can't add anything to a white gesso panel or a good linen canvas and the best oil colours. Today I very often use acrylic colours which, from the point of view of being a stable and enduring medium, are perhaps better than anything the old boys used. One thing I do envy them is that until our modern progressive time, they all used handmade paper which is infinitely more sympathetic than what one buys today. You are told that such and such a paper is handmade – and indeed it is – but by the mile. It lacks that sensitivity and you feel this every time you handle it.

I prefer a half worn-out brush to a new one. Again and again one picks up a brush and the handle bends to the pressure. Through being excited and holding it too tightly, I get a kind of corn on my finger. Any sane man wouldn't have this because there is no need to hold a paint brush so tightly. Eventually the handle becomes curved like a sword blade and that's when I'm happiest. But there's no other mystery to my technique.

Lovers 1969 casein tempera

Fading Ray of Sun 1968 acrylic   AHT

I think that an artist has to go through the whole spectrum. You can't say 'I like blue, I like red'; it sounds fatuous. To me, purple is a melancholy colour and if anything, it is because of one's memories. You feel something ghastly is just over; and the next day, if you are a writer or a painter, and you are able, you do something about it. You don't suddenly swing from something sad to something happy. Your work is everything that you experience.

Latterly because I work more freely and because of this miracle that has happened to me, I can leave a painting to dry and pick up another canvas. Before – and it is far away and long ago – the expense of all these materials worried me desperately; and rather than have several things on the go at once, I preferred to work on one thing, trying to complete it to the utmost. But now, if somebody doesn't like my paintings, I shrug my shoulders and I don't put my foot through them.

I often work on canvas boards because they are very tough and resilient, and you can attack them. I have a whole pile of them now ready to be worked on. I've already toned light and dark reds on some; and a number I've left white because I know that in a week or so I shall know what ground I want. When I visualise a picture, I always – as far as one dare to say anything at all like this – see it in my mind as a complete thing. I think it must be the same for most painters. Here is this space and you see what you are going to paint pretty well 'en masse.' Then it's all rather thinly rubbed in, suggested on the whole surface. Finally I find that, like the sun rising in the east and setting in the west, the entrance to the canvas is somehow to the left.

Since one has been able to put down the last cheque for the ownership of this house, one had felt happier and freer. It's paradise. And of course I think my pictures are freer for it.

Every morning now when I wake up, I think 'My God, isn't it astounding, I owe no man one single penny.' I can't get over it. One has never had so many charming friends – people one really gets on with and a roof which – as far as one can call anything one's own – is one's own. And most important of all, I've enough materials. I just can't believe that today or tomorrow, if I had the energy, I could use up every sheet of drawing-paper in this house; and the next day I would simply go to the paper manufacturer and ask for more. And upstairs there are enough canvasses and paints. That's a thing I've never before had in my life. I can't tell you how important that is for me because now one can quite recklessly go on with one's painting. Before, to pick up a canvas or an expensive sheet of Whatman paper would put the wind up me. And I was always anxious to get something on it. But to be able to use these things more freely is what matters.

It's all so ironical because it is not health or vigour but simply money which has made this possible. When I went, as a youngster, to the National Gallery, I would think, 'Well it's all very well being Velasquez, but how did he buy this huge canvas and where did the paint come from? Being treated like a prince in a king's palace is quite a different story from one's own.' This all sounds so materialistic but often I would go through the National Gallery shaking my head over the expense of making all these pictures.

Latterly through the three exhibitions, I have had some small success. It would have given one's friends and relatives in Amsterdam, who are now dead, great pleasure, a sense of pleasure that even I can't get because one knows one's own faults and what an agonising struggle it has been to paint one decent picture. It would have given them real pleasure after all these years. But it all comes too late. Now I am in this state and I can hardly sleep with excitement. It is so wonderful not to be worried financially. It may be an illusion, but at the moment this idea that I can earn my living by my painting is there. And the very thought makes me delirious.

The Wave 1968 acrylic

A hundred and one things surround and attack me like demons. It is a dance of demons. I've a great longing to do other things; but if I show you my children before they are really there, they won't appear because they are very shy. Afterwards, they won't be because they must be strong enough to withstand the barrage of criticism that will be poured upon their heads. They have to be torn to pieces and walked on and still feel remarkable.

You can come into the workroom. There are a handful of things on the go, but I wouldn't like to discuss them now because it would simply destroy them. I could never bear it if someone stood behind and watched me working. I think it's a much healthier quality not to mind – even to show off if you like. But why I don't show you work in progress is because when it's only half-way through, it looks so entirely different from when it's finished. Then I have had my say and it doesn't matter if we discuss it. It's all an incompleteness – everything. It's nothing more than an approximation. That's why in some ways, I'm sorry when things go and it's farewell. Adieu. Fini.

When you go, I shall try to do something with this and probably I shall be so excited that I shan't be able to do a thing. And it will be ruined. Whereas one has to be quite calm, very collected and with both feet very much on the ground. Your head can be in the clouds. Mine has to be.

Every picture is a failure. If I think of what I have seen and then I think that there is a white canvas; and inside those tubes are colours, it nearly drives me mad to think that what I do is, apparently, the most I can do. One has to go step-by-step. It's fatal to begin thinking about what one has yet to do.

I don't know what makes one less unhappy about one thing than about another. Sometimes I've been stopped in the middle of working by the greengrocer calling. You're alone, so you stagger in with this box. Then you come back to your canvas and perhaps one was so tensed up that the break was a thing from heaven because had one gone on, the picture might well have been ruined. On another occasion you are in your stride when somebody calls and it's absolutely fatuous – a parcel for the neighbour next door or a wrong number – and everything is ruined. It's a little like Coleridge 'In Xanadu did Kubla Khan a Stately Pleasure Dome decree.' You know the story. Coleridge is writing this incredible thing and he is interrupted by the visit of a gentleman from

Stepping Out lithograph

Porlock – which I always think is such a wonderful name – and the whole thing stops like that. I may be quite wrong, but I think that this was an invention by Coleridge because it's so absolutely what happens in life, again and again.

Oasis 1964-65 casein tempera

My happiness is in trying to work. This is in no sense anything original. In fact it's very old-fashioned stuff. I have been asked to write something on my work, but what can I say about painting and drawing? In one way far too much has been said and written about it. And far too few good drawings and paintings exist. It is only when someone like a Cezanne says something that eventually people sit up. In painting one has, at once, to be quite natural and at the same time to know what one wants and why one puts a red there and a green here. It doesn't just come out of a chaotic jumble through hitting a machine in the right place, as in those arcades where you suddenly have a hundred shillings in your hand. I wish I could paint like that – it would be marvellous. But there again it is literally true that the more you cast your bread upon the waters and don't think about anything in return, the more everything springs to life and gives vitality. It's an extraordinary thing. And I've seen it happen again and again.

To me the theme of a little oasis – of this burning – is terrifying. During these last few days, one has been looking through the south windows here at this winter sun. And it has been very, very bright. It is always so much more intense than one manages to make it. Ideas are in one all the time. Sometimes one is uppermost, then a reaction sets in, perhaps because of something that has moved you very deeply. And from that moment, you begin to draw and paint on this particular theme.

The World of Artists

In these past years, the French have thrown up an amazing crowd, for instance Rodin, Maillol, Braque, Matisse, Derain, Bonnard, and Rouault. If you think of Picasso, Soutine, Modigliani and Chagall all coming to Paris where there was this incredible call which made it such an amazing place during those years compared with London.

Chagall is an altogether fascinating fellow. I love the way he has been able to be himself. His inspiration from folk art with the Russian icons and Jewish tradition has been a tremendous thing for him. The pageantry and folklore of it. Think of a black sun by Chagall; or somebody's head knocked off and floating through the sky upside down.

Head in the Clouds lithograph

He's got wonderful fantasy and there is a tremendous freedom and richness in his work. Well, everyone has his timing and link to add. I can see I shall have to steal a black sun from Chagall and send a note to him with apologies. He'd probably paint a blacker sun. An ebony black sun.

The thing that really matters about this whole business of painting is 'How good is the painting?' 'How well is this drawn?' If you look at a 'Mont Saint-Victoire' by Cezanne, then you think 'My God, what a magnificent painting.' I don't start thinking what was going on at the time and whether Cezanne was a symbol of his time. Cezanne's good fortune was that he was free enough to be able to bring to bear his intense, imaginative objectivity.

I think the Cubists were very different men indeed from Cezanne. The movement is interesting and it must have been very exciting for the painters of that moment. But to me, it's a very limited thing. It's like taking a particular small facet; and that's why the movement gradually moves away. One gets a beautiful harmony from the shapes and because of this the work survives. But in relation to Cezanne it was a facet. Greco has that facet in him. And Rembrandt has it. But Rembrandt doesn't say to himself, 'Now with this portrait I'm going to express and stress these planes in this particular way.' What Rembrandt tried to do – there again, think of me trying to put into words what Rembrandt tried to do, really the cheek of it horrifies me – but in fact he tried to plumb the depths as profoundly as he could, in the most natural way.

In relation to the different times, it is interesting to see what happens. In Rembrandt's time, the painters who were really in fashion were the Italianizers. They thought this Italian influence was the hallmark of the greatest beauty. But Rembrandt knew his Titian and Raphael and understood them and the Italians in quite a different way.

Drawing and painting is not just a particular little story, or a fine story or a great story. If it has anything at all, then it is in the drawing and painting itself. And unless the work can show this, it is no good. I have to be alone when I draw and paint; and then I do forget everything. I forget my friends too. But when it is over and I meet them, they are able to keep a straight face and shake hands – the marvellous 'stiff upper-lip' business. 'How do you do?' whereas I overdo it, because I embrace my friends; and frequently to them that's an embarrassment. I go into a workshop and see printers at work; and I could embrace them for being printers or for being good carpenters. I admire a man like Magritte for doing what he did, but I can't put on this mask, this dead-pan screen between me and what I am painting. It has to be at one with me.

My Brother and I lithograph

If you look at a very great master like Jan Van Eyck or Roger Van der Weyden, or Hieronymus Bosch, they are, in a way, just as dead-pan, but they have a terrific passion; and they have this other side of warmth and humanity, so that their work continues to grow and give out in a way that Magritte, to me, does not. An artist has to be all people. He has at once to be absorbed in everything. And yet he must remain objective and above it all.

To do as you please isn't freedom. Very, very gradually through wisdom and experience you become freer. One hopes that as one's experience of life increases, one becomes freer in handling the paint. What is so incredible to me in a man like Rembrandt, is what his late portraits mean in relation to the eyes the old boy had. They're a gift from heaven. Development for the lucky man is something that goes hand-in-hand with his experience.

Different people use a word like 'Freedom' in different ways although perhaps they mean the same thing. If I say that an artist must be free, I literally mean that it's no good my standing in the stale bread queue. That I must have some money and a roof over my head. Of course one must also have the freedom of thought. If you don't have these things, you try and make them.

I hope to become freer and freer. But certainly I have restrained myself in many ways. One has to. Nobody is entirely free in this life. How can they be in relation to other human-beings? I have never consciously wanted to hurt anybody. Because of this lack of something substantial behind me, many things in life have frightened me. One had only to see how Mama behaved to be very frightened indeed, many many times. I think many people associate freedom with what is called 'living dangerously.' I had a friend who again and again told me to live dangerously. I didn't remind him that he was a near millionaire, that I was very much on the other end of the stick; and that the life I was living, compared to his life, was highly dangerous. Every minute of it.

Just imagine living dangerously and let's say – as people so amusingly say – 'making half a million.' What an amazing thought that would be. One can begin to dream of Xanadu and Kubla Khan 'A stately pleasure dome.' It's all a bit late now 'Mon vieux.' My goodness when I think of marvellous chaps like Manet and Renoir. No man is free until he is his own father and his own mother. It is like cutting your own causeway up a mountain, step by step. Perhaps it has happened to me but it's something you don't realise.

Sometimes you are very aware of the symbolism in your work. And sometimes it is a subconscious thing which happens in some strange way whilst one is working. That's why one literally doesn't remember making certain drawings and paintings. If you ask me how I made them, I couldn't tell you. But this has nothing to do with excellence or badness. All these things can be in a great picture. In how it looks. In how the shadow comes. And in how the light falls on the whole thing. It can be a marvellously peaceful symbol, or it can be catastrophic. With Rembrandt, you have only to look at a certain portrait to feel it goes right beyond just looking at a particular head.

There is always a certain struggle in the act of drawing and painting. You may feel very well and very gay, but the memory is of something that happened months ago. And because at that particular moment you are able to look back in comparative tranquillity, you paint that picture.

Since I couldn't earn any money through my work there was, for a very long time, this feeling of an intense and very real guilt. Firstly in relation to helping my mother; and secondly in leaning upon Kate. It was a very unhappy thing for me not to be able to earn my living as a painter. Either you are lucky and strike a happy note in relation to what your contemporaries think is good painting, or you don't. Whereas I think that any painter who has anything in him at all, even if he spends his whole life painting and during that lifetime receives no recognition, is perhaps just as much a symbol of his time.

Dancer lithograph

204

One reads sometimes of the death of a painter or a poet. The poor devil has struggled all his life to write one decent poem or paint a single fine painting. And in fact he doesn't ever really achieve this. There is something very tragic in that. The noble thing is the attempt he made. Miro bought this painting* in the Paris 'flea market.' It is not by a great artist – far from it – but who is to say that this picture has to be enlivened? Miro is a remarkable fellow, but had he had a still greater sensitivity than he has, he would have left the picture alone; and instead have copied it, transforming it with the things that make it absolutely Miro into what he thought it should be. But he should have respected this artist's work.

Top Hat lithograph

The picture is a memorial in relation to this man's death. And Miro should have perhaps painted his own elegy of this monument. But to have destroyed it is, I feel, a profound fault.

April 20th '74

Dear Ricarrdo,

I see the Louvre chiefs are in quite a state about the Picasso gift, and wonder whether he knew that some were fakes, <u>of course he knew</u>! Do they really think that demon genius did not know? He who ransacked the museums of the world and made everything his own of course he was intrigued and enjoyed the joke Ingenius Genius that he was! Sometimes you must go and look at Jan Van Eyck's portrait in the National Gallery called I think the Leal Souvenir (Loyal?) And you will hear the mighty tread of Rembrandt.
Adios old Man. Long live all those who love the Art.

Albertus

Each individual achievement is only a part of the whole. Each one adds what he can. And whether he is genuine is what matters. One sees one's work as a tiny drop in the ocean. Some men have immense genius. A Michelangelo or a Leonardo or an Einstein, well that comes from heaven. But I don't think it is for the man himself to judge. It is only Picasso who has quite convinced himself that he's not just the greatest artist that has ever lived, but that he's shaken the foundations and cracked the building. He is a very extraordinary man. But where I would love and deeply respect certain artists, as I do Memling and Jan Van Eyck, Picasso terrifies me.

*Albert had seen, reproduced in 'The Arts Review', a painting by an unknown artist which Miro had painted over.

Buster lithograph

I think he's quite ruthless. And I wouldn't like to be in his way because if you were, you wouldn't expect to receive anything else but a kick on the pants. He somehow had the power to break away from home and go, as a young man, to Paris; and at once began to fight his way through everything to stand on his own two feet. This last exhibition at the Tate, of his woodcarvings and bronzes and pottery, was remarkable. He is the most ingenious genius. I think another wonderful thing is that through his success and his making money, he broadened his horizon; and his river became all the time wider and wider. And he was able to get a bigger and bigger and more powerful boat. He didn't stop and the money simply meant that he could have his clay models cast into bronze; and that he was able to employ more and more people to print his lithographs and etchings on bigger and bigger paper. I'm all for the artist or anyone else who can use success constructively. Think of this extraordinary business of going to a place where there is a pottery and where things are very down. And simply putting the whole show on its feet again. He is the greatest one-man business in the world. He makes rings round everybody else. His work has enormous vitality. But one feels that a man who makes the things he often does is a very unhappy man.

I think, in one way, it is bound up with our time. He is a tremendous man of the world. And I should think it would be very difficult indeed for him to meet people who are purely disinterested. He has worked very hard to become famous and he's trapped in this. I think he's now reached a very strange point. It's almost as if he has seen it all and knows it all. No man ever can. But sometimes when I look at the later things, it's as if he draws with a certain cynicism. But then that's a long tale in relation to this very remarkable man. This may sound nonsense. And Picasso would be furious if he heard me say this, but I think that early on, somewhere in his heart of hearts, he was profoundly hurt by a woman. It's as if this fantastic fellow – fantastic as he is – has a chip on his shoulder about something that has made him so angry

Painter with Notebook 1968

that he's constantly having to change the situation, whether it's a wife or a style. There's a terrible unhappiness there, and a terrible restlessness if one thinks of the marvellous, ever-more profound development of a Rembrandt.

I seem to remember a story, probably apocryphal, about Pablo. During the invasion, he thought that perhaps it would be a good idea to leave France. I don't myself think that he ever intended to. But this was the story. He looked at the Channel and said 'Oh my God, all that water.' It was quite enough to make him change his mind. And I can imagine that in another way, trees and leaves would get on his nerves as much.

But all the time one comes back to how remarkable and immensely gifted a man Picasso is.

Like every artist he must go on working. Some demon drives him on. His vitality and the ingenuity of his design and thought are absolutely amazing.

Daphne lithograph

As it happens, there has lately been a Rembrandt and a Vincent exhibition. And to me, of course, the world is a more marvellous place for their having been here. Art has nothing to do with being 'a contemporary'; or 'being in advance of one's time.' One could call Rembrandt a man in advance of his time. He's the first really great modern painter and modern psychologist.

Clown in Black Hat lithograph

For me, Rembrandt's late self-portraits are the greatest series of paintings that has ever been painted. One has never seen anything like them. Of all the old boys, Rembrandt is, to me, the most living. It is the character of his work. Unlike a romantic baroque Italian immersed in mythology, he painted the domestic scene. If I see a sheet of marvellous little studies of Saskia or of the household; or his own final dream of a series of self-portraits, it is that which, quite apart from his supreme genius, makes him for me such a living person – more so than a tremendous fellow like Holbein. Holbein left one chalk drawing of himself. It is a wonderful thing. The cool restraint and energyless vitality of this man are quite frightening. But with Rembrandt the door to the room is always open.

In a sense you ask what is impossible to talk about. But let us suppose Rembrandt's life had been one long anthem of success, then the late and more marvellous of the two self-portraits in the National Gallery could not have been painted. *The Conspiracy of the Batavians* must have been absolutely staggering; and those Dutch oxen refused it, telling him to take it away. And now all one has is this fragment in Stockholm. Just think of the mutilation of what must have been one of the greatest pictures ever painted. But Rembrandt was never entirely rejected because commissions did continue until the very end. Like Shakespeare, he had this tremendous genius of understanding for the human situation. And I think his hardships quickened the shaping of what didn't matter. Like a great violinist, he no longer wavered but was able to put it down very simply. I can't imagine Rembrandt wasting any time, ever. But he was only human. I've no doubt that the late things would have become more and more profound. But I think this came about more quickly through the tragedies in his life – just as I think that the death of Titus; and the deaths of all those people whom he had known and loved – this whole procession of disasters that happened so comparatively quickly – eventually killed him.

He was only sixty-three when he died. And I can imagine him at the very end, thinking 'Oh blast' and going on and on. It is impossible not to. His contemporaries threw him overboard and he died very poor. But Rembrandt knew what he had done. If he could have lived to be Frans Hals's age, or Michelangelo's, or Titian's, there would be pictures in this world of which we can't conceive.

In relation to Rembrandt and an infinitely smaller figure, it is only the character of the man which happens to have whatever it is in Nature that makes him a genius, and the other a much smaller figure. But the quality and the feeling and the sincerity are only less to a degree, in relation to the character of the particular man. Rembrandt is so overwhelming that you cannot be an artist – any artist worthy of his salt – and not be influenced by this titanic figure. Other much smaller artists feel this tremendous vibration because of his genius and his passion and his belief.

I worship Rembrandt more than any other painter. And that is simply because I think he is the greatest genius in drawing and painting of the whole lot. And his outlook, to me, is the most marvellously humane and balanced. Yet he worked with untiring passion. Rembrandt, at the end of his life, is the same staggering fellow that he was at the beginning. He simply becomes more and more profound, richer and richer, more and more amazing, always more generous, wider and deeper. It isn't flying from one point to another for the sake of some new idea. It is a tremendous development based upon profound study.

I knew Rembrandt long before I knew Vincent. In many ways Vincent is very different. Yet, in other ways, it amazes me how much alike he is – not because his things are like Rembrandt's in this or that way, but because they are the man's own character and bear the intensity of that character. You have only to look at his marvellous drawings – for instance that back view of an old couple. I could weep with the feeling in those things. The way the man's heels on his poor, pathetic boots have been drawn. It's absolutely like Rembrandt.

One mustn't be afraid of learning from others. And one must be quite frank if another artist has an influence on one. If you look at *The Potato Eaters* and certain English illustrators from the period, like Charles Keene and William Small, whom Vincent adored, it's quite amazing what he learnt from them. The influence is alright if it's genuine, as it was with Vincent. If it's a pastiche, then it's nothing. It was Luke Fildes who drew and had engraved for 'The Graphic' after Dickens's death, *The Empty Chair*. Well, that was where Vincent got his chair picture and Gauguin's empty chair. And Vincent's lithograph *Sorrow*, an incredible piece of work, absolutely based on his experience, has its counterparts in certain engravings. His technique of drawing round a form and then across the back is just like one of these engravers. He admired them intensely, but it's because he feels it intensely that it becomes his own.

It's extraordinary to watch the development of his work. How it becomes more and more his own. How I like *The Sunflowers*. Now they are gay pictures. Vincent would have loved doing them, and have felt that he really was doing his stuff. But I think even Vincent might have been staggered by the queues at his exhibitions now. It's very odd what happens in life. His pictures are so wonderful and their particular wonder cannot really be described. You have to sense it for yourself.

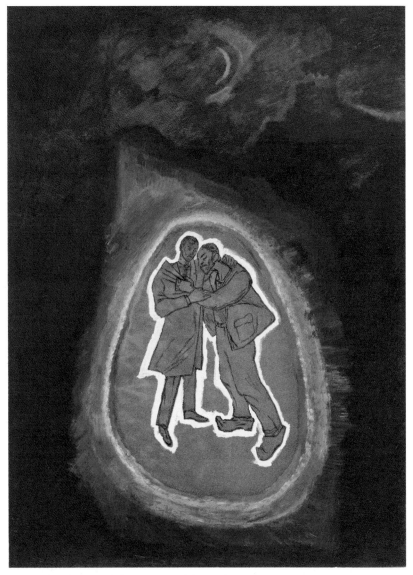

The Meeting of Theo and Vincent Van Gogh in Paradise 1974 acrylic   AHT

If one can imagine Rembrandt and Vincent meeting, I don't think they would have spent much time together. But they would have embraced. They are both the most compassionate of men. And Vincent through his feeling for people and for the whole human situation is, to me, a modern Rembrandt. It is the same blood.

At the Hayward Gallery, Cath and I were going from drawing to drawing. And when we got to the drawing of the *Old Man in a Topper*, there was an old boy with a young man whom I think he was taking round. And the old boy said 'Well now, wouldn't you like to possess one of these things?' The young man said 'No thank you, I would not.' Wonderful. And I looked at the young man and he was rather too exquisitely dressed and altogether rather too polished. And I thought, 'Well, he's being honest about it. From his point of view, he would hate to have one of these drawings.'
The old boy just smiled when he got the reply.

Certainly Vincent was a very emotional man but not so in the superficial sense. When Vincent paints he's a classicist; and the designs are classical. And when he is well, he was absolutely all there. Because he suffered from epilepsy, he had to drive himself to work; and to get something done. Like every great man he had a lot to say, and his situation must have been terrible beyond belief. Thank God for Rembrandt, he didn't have that.

And Rembrandt sparked from the very beginning as being someone different.
Also one can see by the way he paints his mother and father and sister, that he's really quite a happy young man. And the family are reasonably well off. Whereas Vincent was deeply troubled about being a terrible burden to Theo. That in itself was an agonising situation. All this was a tremendous strain upon Vincent. And sometimes one sees that in a way it damages certain pictures. But most of them shine through. From the beginning, one sees the intensity and sincerity of the man. And then gradually, the greater and greater freedom. He dies when he is thirty-seven, having done what he did in just over ten years.

There is no doubt that Van Gogh loved. But the terrible intensity of his character frightened women. They were terrified of this passionate man; and I can understand why. To them – and perhaps they were right – he was half-mad. Anybody who is as passionate about painting as he was must be. Certainly poor Vincent caught it in the neck because of this – not because he didn't want to lead a sane and normal life as a married man. He did and says so again and again. I think Vincent's case was tragic. But I think Vincent being made as he was would, in any event, have had his own troubles. The inevitability of his life is like a Greek tragedy. It was his particular intensity that eventually made things impossible for him. He really did believe. And it is because of his belief and compassion that his work moves people so much.

White Face, Braided Hat lithograph

If one has, as I have, an intense and profound admiration and love for Rembrandt and Vincent, then it is something to do with one's own life. It's as if one day you read a fine author of the past and have pleasure in finding that this author and you have the same thought. It is as though there are affinities so that when you try to draw and paint what is real and true to you, it has a connection with other things.

This change is only a beginning to me. If I look at some of the last things, I think I see in them a greater freedom but they're still not free enough. They must all become richer through greater and greater understanding.

Again and again one says 'Thank God my pictures are bought,' because quite apart from being able to settle one more bill, I think that bought pictures are more likely to be looked after. But very often they're bought or praised for the wrong reasons. I have had said to me in various and different ways, 'Oh, I loved your drawing – the red chalk went exactly with the red in the carpet.' Then flaming bill or no flaming bill, you're not so happy. One newspaper critic wrote about my work 'The necrophilic unpleasantness of the best expressionism is missing, making most of these canvasses quite cheerful and colourful, but they are assured and consistent.'

White Face in Straw Hat lithograph

Well he's missed the whole point. There is a small 'Crucifixion' by Antonello da Messina in the National Gallery, painted on a very clear bright day. And because of that it has a peculiar terribleness. It was also curious that nobody talked about this odd point of the rock.

One critic honoured me by writing – and I was delighted to read this headline – 'The Originality of Albert Houthuesen.' Never in my life have I thought of being original. I have only looked at the sea and the land and the sky. I have looked at the marvellous men and women one sees. And I have gone to the theatre. It is such an astounding world to look at. Everything in Nature is admirable, everywhere and all the time. And all I have wanted to do is to try and paint what I had seen, either in a dream or in reality.

Any painter is a very lucky man if, during his life, a handful of people really stop to look at his work. It would be amusing to think that one's work was known to many people but I wouldn't forget that only half-a-dozen really knew about it.

The last time I was looking at the Velasquez *Rokeby Venus* in the National Gallery, a woman passed in front of me sucking a toffee. It interested her far more than the Velasquez. She was filled with toffee – in fact she was entirely made of toffee. Well, I feel abashed and saddened by this kind of thing and in a way abused too. When I was at the Vincent show at the Hayward, it was the thing to see Vincent. So hundreds of school-children were looking at the Vincents. The time they finished work at school was the time for knocking off from the Gallery; and whilst they were inside there were fights; and where I happened to be, were a couple of youngsters kicking a case around. And of course they were quite right. The real place for these children was outside; and if a few wanted to look at these things then let them. Heaven knows, amongst those children there perhaps might be, in his or her own way, another Vincent; and that child will remember. But there will only be one or two who do. To thousands it doesn't mean anything. And this crazy totting up of numbers in relation to exhibition attendances is meaningless. You can't make anybody worship these things. If a horse doesn't want to drink it won't. And if people don't want to go to the National Gallery or to the Tate,

I see no reason why they should. I've talked with my good friend the newsagent here. He is a very nice chap and he lives on the doorstep of the Dulwich Art Gallery; but he's never been inside. Every evening we have great jokes about this. He knows I'm trying to draw and paint and he's very intrigued that somebody should be such an ass as to go on trying. He knows the name of Rembrandt but he's never been inside the gallery because it's far more important for him, after a long day's work, to get back to his wife and children and have his dinner. And from his point of view, he's absolutely right.

One or two people have said they believe that the things I have produced will survive. I have now had three exhibitions which means that a conservative estimate of a hundred and fifty drawings and paintings have been shown. And not a single museum has thought it worthwhile buying one of them. It doesn't really matter, but if you have loved and worked at something all your life, it's very odd to find that in relation to any sort of general acknowledgement, there hasn't been the slightest flicker of an eyelid. The Tate has three of my pictures, and a drawing. They live in cellars and lead this very exclusive, carefully-guarded life. One day, they will have, one hopes, the vulgar gaze of the multitude.

One has the belief that the work will survive. But then I have this other terrible realisation that since a canvas is only a piece of linen, and paint is only paint; and since one sees what happens in the world, I see the whole thing dissolve into dust. And sometimes this makes it impossible for me to work. One paints because one has to, although it is almost a fantasy to do so. If I really wanted my work to survive then I should cast it in bronze.

Last Will and Testament 1966

Pills Yet More Pills 1961-63

Pills Yet More Pills

What is hardest is when very early on you try to stand on your own two feet and do what you instinctively feel you want to do; and you receive no encouragement but only criticism. It's like something undermined. Suppose I had had a son; and I thought 'This boy is a born clown or he dances when there is music.' Well somehow one would have seen to it – even if one had no money – that he could have followed whatever had been his bent. But if that something is damned-up like a river and it's 'No, no, no' the whole time, then eventually it makes you ill.

I have such an intense desire to paint. One must simply brush aside everything that is irrelevant and try to work. I would most certainly die if I couldn't. But I could kill myself very easily by overworking. This thing I have about 'As well as I can.' At the moment I'm dissolving this tiny pill. Some people have pills to make things psychedelic and pep them up. I take them to pipe me down.

You see it's six o'clock now and I'm just beginning to wake up. I've got all these pills inside me. And if I don't take them, apparently I shall explode. The more of these pills you take, the more you sleep, the slower your reactions are; and the swifter time appears to pass.

I always have a feeling of sadness when the longest day of the year has just passed and the days grow shorter. Now it is spring I feel a tremendous elation. I see there are little buds on this rose creeper and I know the days are growing longer. And somehow one is able to do more work. As it becomes twilight, you put a canvas aside and the very dimness of the light begins to pull it together again; and you see it in another light.

Unfortunately the painter needs daylight and the lateness of my waking up every day now makes me furious. I'd love to have the strength and vitality to take it all in my stride. I like the morning but it's true that I've always woken up at night. If one had a son whom you trained from very early on to be sensible, the first years he would live a cabbage-like existence, so that the child was not too excited and not too sad nor too gay. That would be the ideal thing. Then one's body would work as it should and you wouldn't, for the rest of your life, have to suffer from duodenal ulcers, migraines and high blood-pressure. You may think I have this business of my health on the brain but it is such a drag on me that I don't know how I can ever hope to do remotely what I want to. Since we came to this house, I have learnt more and more how to make the most of my time and not to waste it. It means that I don't go out to the ballet or the theatre because if I do, I'm knocked out the next day.

Look what a beautiful day it's been today and yesterday and the day before. We've had a marvellous light. And what a wonderful thing it would be to be able to walk into one's work-room at nine o'clock, at the latest, when already half the day has gone for some people; and work up to the time we met this afternoon, instead of being this drugged layabout. Who wants to be that?

I'm upset when sometimes I get worked up too late. In this way I'm a very unwise man. I begin to look through a book, perhaps on Matisse or Delacroix or Signorelli, and then of course I can't sleep. Whereas I wish I could turn on the telly and watch a marvellous clown, laugh my head off, and sleep like a log. But one turns on the telly and often it is such unutterable rubbish that one just groans in despair.

All I want now is a good night's sleep and as early a day as possible, hoping and praying for a very good light. Then perhaps another patch will be added to today's thing and then another.

What is the Time? lithograph

One ought to be as strong as a cart-horse instead of like a fly. And on Monday, getting ready, in fear, for the dentist. And on Tuesday 'Aaaaaaaah!' 'I beg your pardon, I'm so sorry.' 'Oh, it's quite alright – now.'

At first I had dreaded going to the dentist because of the literally barbaric methods I had had the misfortune to experience. And now I meet this charming man with his modern anaesthetics, and one gets through it. He told me I had what he called 'long-boned teeth,' and yesterday, to my amazement, I heard him say, 'Hold his hand, nurse.' So I 'Ah, ah!!' said to him afterwards, 'You've taken out thirty teeth and this is the first time you've said 'Hold his hand.' 'It's an absolute shame.' So next Tuesday, I shall say, 'Nurse, come along – hand please,' for she is a charming girl. This modern surgery is marvellous and I strongly advise you to go immediately and have all your teeth out.

The extraordinary thing I've noticed with doctors is their real curiosity and interest in the art of painting. 'Do you paint landscape or do you paint still-life?' or 'Which is the most difficult?' The man who makes a wonderful diagnosis or who carries out an operation is an artist. Good doctors are just like good painters and I've always wanted to give something to every doctor I've known – and their assistants.

The World Upside Down

Every man is destined to be from birth what his character makes him. And finally one is what one is because of everything that surrounds one. I can't sit down and paint that exquisite little plant in a mood of happiness. How can I? One is simply not living in the fifteenth or sixteenth century. I go out of the house and instead of walking along a country lane, I walk along a paved street. I can think of certain beautiful things by Vermeer – to take a man of the utmost genius – and in one sense you cannot imagine a Vermeer being painted today. It sounds absurd because one can. But it would be different. Although I intensely admire Boucher and Fragonard, I couldn't possibly paint in the same spirit. If I look at a *Fête Champêtre* by Watteau, I see its compact of tragedy. His depth of feeling is remarkable. And it is amazing to me how he sees and understands the other side of life and is able to express it.

Just now you mentioned the Laughton film, and Rembrandt in the film talking about his love for Saskia. Well, I know a little etching by Rembrandt where he is full-face and very close to the spectator; and there is a little Saskia just behind. This was drawn very soon after their marriage and it is incredible how these things are not really read. People talk about the intense happiness of Rembrandt and Saskia. Of course they were in love and he was deeply moved. But really early on, something went wrong. You have only to look behind at what is in those etched lines, and at the head of Rembrandt, to see that some appalling thing has happened. And I think it was Saskia's ill-health.

It is fantastic to think how little one knows about one's own destiny. One could discuss it for hours but I really don't have the sort of energy to go into it. As a purely personal feeling, I think that with many things I have been unlucky.

World Upside Down 1966-67

And in this I would put my health first. I mean, what is the time now? Twenty-past five and I am literally only just beginning my day. What a disaster. And how dreary it is. But it's useless to say 'I've been an unlucky fellow.' The miracle is that I've had the luck to be able to try and do what I wanted to do, with a roof over my head and food on the table. My great disappointment is in the shortcomings of my work. What a vanity it is to have this agony over one's work. I can't even bear to say 'I have done my best.' I haven't. I've had certain chances and if I haven't painted something which I can call my best, then it is my fault. It is extraordinary that one can love something – in my case painting – so much; and yet because of it have to go through such anguish.

I find this whole business of why one is a painter very difficult to explain. Certainly if you insist on being a painter and then go through hell, I see no reason why you should be pitied. None at all. It is so absolutely marvellous to try to draw and paint. Every time I take a canvas and begin to put out the colours, it is inexplicably wonderful and I am always so inexplicably happy.

Head in a Niche lithograph

Every morning I pick up 'The Times' and 'The Telegraph'. And every morning I am appalled at the state of the world. It is an absolute veil of tears. I have never known anything other than an insane, tragic situation going on in some part of the world. And I believe that one's work is all in relation to how you feel about these things.

Never before has there been anything so monstrous. People have always murdered each other. Again and again people have gone to war; and the villages have been torn to pieces and the women raped. But they've never actually polluted the very atmosphere to such an extent that man is signing his own death warrant.

When I start a drawing or painting, I have this feeling that inevitably it will turn to dust. I can literally see it as dust. I know that the things in the National Gallery, the Van Eycks, the Rembrandts, the Velasquez will all be nothing. It will all pass away. So what the devil can you do?

I made one or two things I called *House of Cards* and *World Upside Down*. The implications are appalling because I know what it is to try and build up something and then to simply have it knocked from under your feet so that before you can turn round, everything has gone. These were serious things without any sense of happiness or gaiety. And I thought 'Well, these are very personal and I should like to keep them.' Yet I also thought that because of the subject they would be unsaleable. The extraordinary thing is that one or two have gone to people who have literally had everything knocked away from under them. And this is the other thing about drawing or painting, writing or whatever it is, that if you manage to express something which you have experienced and felt, it sometimes touches other people. That in itself is something you cannot equate with measurements or with a self-conscious attitude about things. If I were going to say 'Now I shall paint something really tragic and moving,' it would be completely false to do so.

Understudy lithograph

Poet 1967

Sometimes my own things frighten me. This does. To me it is as if he has seen every disaster. Last night on the telly, I heard the Jewish cantor Koussevitzky. You listen to that man, and you see the film the Germans – these particular 'last solution' people – made of the siege of Warsaw. And it's heart-breaking. Once you've seen something like that, you can't forget it. It's so unbelievably horrible. It's criminal the way that human-beings can behave. How can they? And at the same time you know that in the world these terrible things are happening. I can't stand a man like Napoleon. The Napoleons or the Caesars are, as far as I'm concerned, all in the same bag. What does all this business of power and ambition and success mean? It's all politics. It's terrifying to see the jealously that goes on around one. But apparently sane and reasonable people have these particular qualities – so help the others. I think perhaps the normal human-being growing up is all these things. Gradually you learn more and you develop. And you are as reasonable as you can be.

Pelléas and Mélisande 1967

It is difficult to talk about, and that is crudely put. Man has these two sides. One thinks of the incredible genius of mankind, and yet one sees the ghastly way in which it can be used. Just think what a world this could be if every human-being could behave at least reasonably. I have met doctors and nurses who are very dedicated people and do a great deal of good. Working in this way has made them happier people; so it is really a very simple and direct thing.

I met and fell in love with Kate. You fall in love, you are young and willy-nilly you marry. I can very easily imagine myself living and working alone and quite possibly, eventually not taking too much care of myself. But I cannot imagine not being in love. I should consider that to be a most dreary and melancholy state.

The other evening, I was listening on the telly to a young artist giving a talk on Renoir. He talked about the little nudes, exquisite little nudes they are to me. And one got the feeling from him that Renoir painted far too many of these things. 'Bathing Women' this way, that way, back-view, front-ways. Renoir, as far as I'm concerned, couldn't paint too many naked women. It was absolutely Renoir. He had to do this; and through these studies gradually come some absolute masterpieces. Friends have told me that there are too many Turners in the Tate. If there were twice the number, there still wouldn't be too many.

I can't see it that way. It's a misconception. Renoir made dozens of these small studies. But this young man didn't see the point. In other words, he can't love to the extent that Renoir was in love with his idea. It was Renoir's theme in life – one vast hymn to Nature and the beauty of women. Whether he paints melons or grapes or the sun or flowers or women, that was Renoir. And thank God it was.

One listens to music and, to me, it is something so close to painting that, quite without knowing it, there is an electric affinity. I had a letter from a friend saying how like Sibelius he found some of my work. Well, that has never crossed my mind. When I listen to Handel or to Bach, I think primarily of something noble and grand. It excites me terribly. When I listen to Sibelius and to Chopin – and there is no-one I love more than Chopin – I have sometimes thought what a wonderful thing it would be if one could paint pictures using literally colour alone to convey these things that move me to tears. I find it so difficult to listen to music because if I listen to Sibelius or to Chopin then, before I know it, I'm in tears. And I'm thankful I'm alone because no-one sees me weeping and I can just about get through it. With Kate we both weep and I have to turn it off.

Chopin inscribed: *This evening 28th June 1960*

221

Black Rock 1966

I seem to remember reading that Vincent, listening to music, was far more interested
in how the musicians looked than in their music. Yet his work is absolutely musical.
And Turner's work is like looking at music. One day I am determined – I who cannot
play a note on the piano – to get a really super grand. And I shall go on my knees
and I shall say to your friend, 'For Heavens sake, come here and play this piano.
And make it as hot as you can.'

I don't think I would have thought of any musician, had I been on the other side of the
moon. I would have been too stunned by this leaden blackness and quite terrified. In spite
of having seen it on the telly and heard the voices of the astronauts, I still can't believe
that it has happened. It's all so incredible. But having seen these marvellous photographs
of the moon and those of the earth – which in a way interest me more – it's still here
that I want to be.

Just think of being able to sit in this little garden and over there is Ruskin Park.
And a little way beyond is Dulwich Park. And if I get onto a bus, then in half-an-hour,
I'm inside the National Gallery looking at a Velasquez or a Rembrandt that I was perhaps
thinking about.

Tea, Love Walk

I still feel I haven't really seen the master-pieces in the National Gallery and in the Victoria and Albert. They are all treasure troves to be found. I have looked many times, but I've only looked superficially. If I think of the Greek vases in the British Museum, I couldn't say I really knew them. And I can still walk through London an absolute stranger. For me, travel is a time-waster, but since I can't do it, I suppose I put up this defence. However I would far prefer to really know my own back-garden than make a quick tour of Italy – to really get to know this mulberry tree which I look at everyday and still don't begin to understand. Look at this rose which I still can't begin to paint. The more I look at it, the more amazing it becomes.

There would be no point in my now travelling three times round the world or going off to the South Pole. By the way, look at this paper-napkin which I've twisted. It's just like an iceberg. Or an Arab. Or the torn-up root of an old tree.

Cleft Tree lithograph

223

Rain 1968 acrylic

The world is such an incredible place. And for an enquiring mind, it is so mysterious and wonderful that there is no time to be bored. It enthrals me from the moment I awake. When one says one hopes to make one's work more cosmic it sounds arrogant, but it is only what painters are trying to do all the time. If you look at Michelangelo's ceiling or Vincent's *Reaper*, you can see that they are all conscious of these intense affinities in Nature. In everything. Everywhere.

Richard Nathanson

I took these photographs one glorious afternoon in July 1969 and was later struck by how close, in animated feeling and spirit, they were to Buziau.

The Beginning of Other Things

Clown Conjurer c.1967 watercolour and collage

Aren't we past the shortest day? Yes we are. Every day is another couple of minutes' daylight. It's marvellous. Spring is on the way, my dear Richard. In a week or so, you will see the trees covered with a haze of green. It is always such a miracle to me. But Nature doesn't stop and think about this. It is there all the time, growing and growing. You look out of this window, and see very young pigeons who have just fallen out of the nest. And you can't so much as go by before you see the same birds become rather more aggressive amongst each other; and begin to spread their wings.

Hope 1968 acrylic

Every painter knows what he has done. But the difficult thing about life is that you are not yourself until you are your own father. In spite of whatever Fate holds in store, you must stand on your own two feet. Not until that time do you fully become yourself; or are you able to express the potential that is within you, however humbly. One has an absolute duty to do one's best. But no artist can go beyond what he can do. He can only work with the greatest love he has.

A person's development is a very long and mysterious process. Very, very gradually, through wisdom and experience, you become freer. You can't pinpoint a particular stage of development. You weep more. You laugh more. You are older. And somehow you have changed. I don't think a painter is anything other than an instrument; and how he does it he cannot really explain. The brush in your hand takes over and you don't even know you're painting.

Walk to the Moon, Childhood Command 1967-69

Anyone who is concerned with doing a thing as well as it can be done, during this brief vale of tears, is perhaps saved many temptations. This is because of an absolute value. People can be marvellously articulate about a philosophical idea. A profound religion can be split into many facets. But finally it all comes down to being as reasonable as one can. And to doing the job as well as one can, in everything.

My work is a world only touched. And to carry on is far more important than anything else. I feel this is the beginning of other things, another sort of happiness. My drawings and paintings are all steps and I don't go back on them. They are part of one's restrictions and part of one's little gift. They are absolutely part of you because with every step you take, you don't think about believing in it, you do believe in it. Yet I should like to paint things which are so rich and intense that they will annihilate what has gone before.

One can only paint anything at all, whatever the subject, through knowing it. And one must love it and be moved more than one can say; and certainly more than I care to talk about. In a sense nothing in art can be explained. And the only talking that is worth talking is drawing and painting. The irony is to be well enough just to live long enough.

The Fall of Icarus and The Triumph 1971-72 acrylic

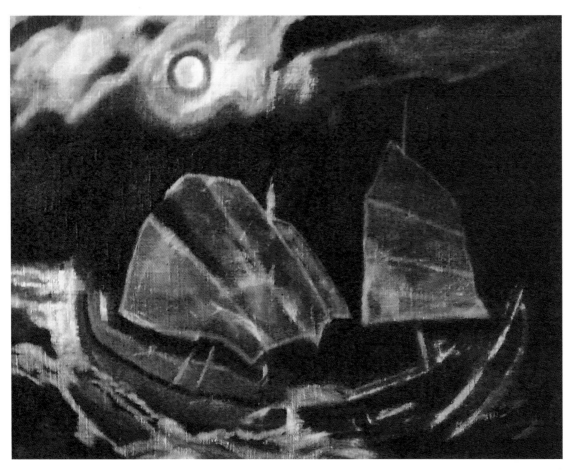

Elegy to Lost Fishermen 1973 acrylic

Dreaming Clown 1974-75 acrylic

AHT

Carnival Kings 1974 acrylic

AHT

St Philemon, Painted Horse and Clowns 1974-75 acrylic

AHT

Moon, Muse and Poet Clown 1972-73 acrylic

AHT

White-Faced Clown against Cavernous Backcloth 1972 acrylic

Bouquet in a Pottery Jar 1973 acrylic

Smiling Clown 1974 acrylic

Aunt Sally's Sister 1973 acrylic

Clown with Broad-brimmed Hat 1978 acrylic

Walk To The Moon, Childhood Admonishment 1975 acrylic   AHT

Fisherman and Burning Bush 1963-73

ALBERT HOUTHUESEN
1903-1979

1903   Born 3rd October at 263 Albert Cuyp Straat, Amsterdam.
Christened Albertus Johannes Houthuesen.

1911   Father dies on 5th November.

1912   Moves to London with his mother, sister, and two brothers. Mother sets up a boarding house at 20 Constantine Rd, Hampstead. Albert attends Fleet Rd Elementary School.

1917-23   Already delivering groceries after school and on Saturdays when he leaves school in 1917. Begins evening classes at St Martin's School of Art. Visits the great London museums. Becomes a full-time grocer's assistant; then a lens grinder, apprentice engraver, tailor's stencil cutter, furniture restorer; and designer of lettering on architectural stones.

1919   Shares a studio in Howland Street with Barnett Freedman, Gerry Ososki and Reginald Brill, fellow students at St Martin's.

1921   First of three brief visits to Holland.

1922   First attempt at the Royal College of Art scholarship. Becomes a naturalized British citizen.

1923   Second scholarship attempt.

1924   Awarded an £80 annual scholarship to the Royal College of Art. Henry Moore, Barbara Hepworth, Edward Burra, Ceri Richards and Cecil Collins are among his fellow students.

1927   For diploma, paints *Supper at Emmaus* which Cecil Collins later said 'Touched a mystical stream, a manifestation of a higher form of consciousness.'
Meets Catherine Dean in the autumn.

1928   Stays on at College as a student demonstrator. Leaves on 20th July and takes up a poorly paid evening teaching post at the Mary Ward Settlement Working Men's College. Spends a fortnight in the Cotswalds with the Rothensteins. At Christmas, he and Catherine are officially engaged. Takes two small top rooms in Savernake Rd, using the front room as a studio.

1929   Evening classes pay a pittance.
Undertakes the first of his commissions for the Duke of Bedford (again in 1933, 1936, 1937, and 1938). Sees the Diaghilev Ballet 'Le Tricorne' with the original Picasso sets and costumes.

Catherine leaves the Royal College of Art and takes a teaching post in Manchester. Albert remains in London, staying with the Rothensteins before moving back to Constantine Rd.

1930   Catherine (with an annual salary of £130) takes Albert and her mother for a fortnight's holiday in the Lake District.

1931   Albert and Catherine marry on 3rd October. And rent rooms at 20 Abbey Gardens, St John's Wood.

1932   The first of many sojourns in the mining village of Trelogan, North Wales.
Also visits Devon and Sussex and paints his first seascapes.

1935   Catherine suffers a miscarriage.

1936   Albert is very ill with a duodenal ulcer.

1937   Begins work on the Duchess of Bedford's memorial window (completed in 1938).

1938   Move to studio flat in 37b Greville Rd, St John's Wood.

1940   Bombing badly damages their home. Damp subsequently destroys over forty paintings placed in war-time storage. Albert is rejected by the army on health grounds. And becomes a tracer at the London North East Railway draftsmen's office in Doncaster.

1944	His 'war work' leads to a severe nervous breakdown. Meets the Hermans, a family of Russian Jewish musical clowns and makes his first clown drawings.
1945	Returns penniless to London in July. And becomes a warden at a student hostel in the Elephant and Castle. Receives first treatment for high blood-pressure. Visits the ballet many times.
1948	Last stay in Wales.
1950	Autumn move to Stone Hall, Oxted in Surrey.
1952	Moves to first (and last) home, in Love Walk, Camberwell, southeast London.
1961	First one-man exhibition, in May, at the Reid Gallery, London. Has operation in June.
1963	Second exhibition at Reids.
1964	Victor Waddington becomes his representative.
1966	Mother dies, aged ninety-two.
1967	Represented by the Mercury Gallery who hold third exhibition. Albert and Richard Nathanson begin their conversations.
1974	Richard Nathanson becomes Albert's representative and, over the next five years, arranges seven exhibitions of his work.
1977	BBC broadcast the documentry *Walk to The Moon* on Albert's life and work.
1979	Albert dies at home on 20th October.

Albert Houthuesen's Work is in the following Museums:

The Ashmolean Museum, Oxford.
The British Museum, London.
Carlisle Museum and Art Gallery.
Museums, Sheffield.
Leeds Art Gallery.
National Museum of Wales, Cardiff.
Nottingham City Art Gallery.
Royal Air Force Museum, Hendon.
Stoke-on-Trent City Museum and Art Gallery.
Tate Britain, London.
The Theatre Museum, London.
Ulster Museum, Belfast.
Victoria & Albert Museum, London.

Bibliography

John Rothenstein	'British Art since 1900', 1962.
John Rothenstein	'Albert Houthuesen: An Appreciation' 1969.
John Rothenstein	'Modern English Painters', volume 3, 1974.
David Buckman	'Artists in Britain since 1945', 2006.

List of Illustrated Works

Unless otherwise stated, the painting medium is oil. And drawing medium 'conté crayon'.

Inches precede centimetres.

Lithograph measurements relate to the furthermost marks made by the artist.

64. Follower of St Philemon, lithograph; 23 x 16 (58.4 x 40.6).

67. Italian Model c.1925, pencil; 22 x 15 (55.9 x 38.1). Skeleton Waving 1919, pencil; 16 ¼ x 6 ½ (41.2 x 16.5).

68. Seated Model 1923, pencil; 13 ¾ x 9 ¾ (35 x 24.8) Madame Paul c.1924, ink; 14 ½ x 5 ¼ (36.9 x 13.3).

69. Toupet, lithograph; 17 x 8 ¼ (43.1 x 20.9).

70. Supper at Emmaus 1927; 30 x 41 ½ (76.4 x 105.5).

71. Clown Saint, lithograph; 21 ½ x 16 ¾ (54.6 x 42.5).

72. Walker's Butchers 1930, charcoal, white chalk; 22 x 30 (55.9 x 76.2).

74. Catherine 1934, pencil; 31 x 22 ½ (78.8 x 57.2).

77. Apple Head 1928, ink; 8 7/8 x 6 7/8 (22.5 x 17.5).

78. The Journey 1927; 36 x 48 (91.5 x 122).

79. Mountainous Landscape 1926-30, ink and charcoal; 21 ½ x 30 ¼ (54.6 x 76.9).

80. Hampstead Heath 1931; 11 3/8 x 14 1/8 (28.9 x 35.8).

81. Self-Portrait 1929, pencil, black chalk; 27 3/8 x 20 ½ (69.7 x 52).

82. Celebration, coloured lithograph; 14 ¾ x 12 (37.4 x 30.5).

83. 'Out of Work Men' – six drawings c.1932, pencil and ink; approximately 11 ¾ x 9 ½ (29.8 x 24.1).

84. Self-Portrait 1930, charcoal, white chalk; 22 x 30 (55.9 x 76.2). Lavender Seller 1931, pencil; 15 ¾ x 10 ¼ (40 x 26). Scotland Road, Liverpool 1932, sepia ink; 15 ¾ x 12 ½ (40 x 31.8).

85. Beachy Head 1932, 8 x 10 (20.2 x 25.3). King Lear 1931, ink; 22 ¾ x 17 ¾ (57.8 x 45.1).

86. The Stack Yard 1935, 36 x 48 (91.5 x 122).

87. Rocky Coast 1935, watercolour, ink; 18 ½ x 24 ½ (47 x 61.6). Miner 1935, watercolour; 11 ½ x 9 ½ (29.2 x 24.1).

88. Miner 1938, 30 x 25 (76.2 x 63.5).

89. William Jones 1933, 26 ¾ x 19 ½ (68 x 49.5).

90. Miner c.1935, charcoal; 23 ¾ x 17 ¾ (60.5 x 45.1).

91. Jones Whitehorse 1934; 48 x 36 (122 x 91.5).

93. Painted in a Village - Harry Jones 1933; 36 x 26 ¾ (91.5 x 68).

94. William Price Lloyd 1937; 92 x 40 (233.8 x 101.7).

96. Jo Parry 1935; 48 x 36 (122 x 91.5).

98. Young Collier c.1935; 23 ¾ x 19 (60.3 x 48.2).

99. John Savage c.1935; 27 x 20 (68.5 x 50.7).

100. Barn, Berthengam 1934; 28 x 36 (78.1 x 91.5).

101. Catherine Recovering from Illness 1935, ink; 14 x 10 (35.5 x 25.4). The Mad Sailor c.1935, pencil; 10 ½ x 8 ½ (26.7 x 21.5).

102. Apples in an Old Felt Hat 1936; 25 x 30 (63.5 x 76.2).

103. Memorial Window, 1937-38. Reproduced by kind permission of His Grace the Duke of Bedford & the Trustees of the Bedford Estates.

104. Woburn Matthias 1936; 24 ½ x 29 ½ (62.2 x 75).

105. Sea Skull 1938; 11 x 13 (28 x 33).

106. Convolvulus 1939; 28 x 36 (71.1 x 91.4).

107. Winter 1940, 121 ¾ x 71 ½ (309.4 x 181.7).

108. Catherine 1940, crayon; 21 x 15 ½ (53.3 x 39.3).

109. Yew Tree and Sheep's Skull, begun 1938; 28 x 36 (71.1 x 91.4).

110. Dead Sparrow Hawk 1939; 22 x 26 (55.9 x 66).

111. Crown of Thorns 1940; 35 ½ x 47 ½ (90.2 x 120.7).

112. Christ Mocked 1940-60, charcoal; 30 x 24 (76.2 x 61).

113. Christ Mocked 1939, ink; 15 ¾ x 11 7/8 (40 x 30.3).

114. The Apple Branch 1940; 27 ½ x 35 ½ (60.8 x 90.2).

115. Voyage 1940-54; 36 x 48 (91.5 x 122).

116. Acrobat Clown, lithograph; 16 ½ x 11 ¼ (41.9 x 28.5). Punch Drunk Bruiser, lithograph; 24 x 20 (60.9 x 50.8).

117. Laurelled Head 1941, charcoal; 30 x 22 (76.2 x 55.9).

118. Christ Mocked 1941, charcoal; 26 x 18 (66 x 45.7).

119. White Face, Black Necktie, lithograph; 23 x 18 (58.4 x 45.7).

120. Tracing - Pressed Dome and Cover (double-riveted) 1943, ink.

121. Busker with Dog, lithograph; 19 ¼ x 14 ½ (48.8 x 36.8).

123. Hubbub, lithograph; 23 x 17 7/8 (58.4 x 45.4).

124. Three Years Hell 1944, watercolour; 11 x 9 ¼ (28 x 23.5).

125. Christ Mocked 1943, charcoal; 29 x 21 ¼ (73.7 x 54).

126. Head, lithograph; 14 ½ x 10 ¼ (36.8 x 26).

127. Herbert Houthuesen c.1943; 35 ¼ x 27 3/8 (89.5 x 69.5).

128. Somnambulist 1943-66, watercolour; 30 ½ x 22 (77.5 x 55.9).

129. Anvil 1943-66, watercolour, collage;
30 ½ x 22 (77.5 x 55.9).

130. Farmer Bramley's Prize Gelding 1944;
30 x 40 (76.2 x 101.7).

131. Three Clown Heads 1944, ink; 18 ¾ x 13 (47.7 x 33).

132. Michel Herman's 19 inch shoes 1944;
10 x 14 (25.4 x 35.5).
Michel Herman 1944, pencil; 14 ¼ x 10 (36.2 x 25.3).
Danny Polo 1944, ink; 15 ½ x 11 ¼ (39.4 x 28.5).

133. Charles Cameron 1945, ink;
19 ¾ x 14 1/8 (50.2 x 35.8).

134. Danny Polo 1945, ink; 15 ½ x 11 ¼ (39.4 x 28.5).

135. Prisoner's Garland 1940-46, 40 x 30 ¼ (101.7 x 76.9).

136. Laura, coloured lithograph; 19 ¾ x 15 (50.1 x 38.1).

137. Italian Peaches 1947, 19 ½ x 13 ½ (49.5 x 34.3).
Another Princess, lithograph; 19 ¾ x 15 (50.2 x 38.1).

138. Near Borough High Street c.1946, ink;
10 x 14 (25.4 x 35.5).
Undertones of War 1945-46, charcoal;
28 x 36 (71.1 x 91.4).

139. Pomegranates 1946; 17 ¼ x 21 ¼ (43.8 x 54).

140-144. Ana Nevada, 18 sketchbook studies 1946,
pencil, ink & wash.
sheet size 8 ¼ x 5 ¼ (21 x 13.3).
Dancer and Duena, ink; 11 3/8 x 9 1/8 (29 x 23).

145. Duena and Dancer 1947, pencil;
10 ½ x 8 ½ (26.7 x 21.6).
Duena 1947, ink and gouache;
11 3/8 x 9 1/8 (29 x 23).
Duena and Dancer 1947, ink;
14 x 10 (35.5 x 25.4).

146. Castinets c.1949; 8 x 12 (20.3 x 30.5).

148. Ana Nevada 1950, 31 x 22 (78.8 x 55.7).

149. Tricorne, lithograph; 17 ½ x 17 ¼ (44.4 x 43.8).

150. Clown Conjurer c.1949, conté, collage;
29 ¾ x 19 ¾ (75.5 x 50.2).
Tiny Hat, lithograph; 18 ½ x 13 (47 x 33).

151. Melons 1945; 26 x 35 (66 x 88.9).

152. Cedar Tree 1952; 21 x 30 (53.3 x 76.2).

153. Roses 1952; 30 x 25 (76.2 x 63.5).
Vision of St Eustace c.1950, pencil;
28 x 20 ½ (71.1 x 52.1).

154. Daffodils and Magnolia in Enamel Jug 1952;
30 x 25 (76.2 x 63.5).

155. Wrestler Charlie, lithograph;
22 ¾ x 17 ¾ (57.7 x 45.1).
Sea Shell, lithograph (not initialled);
15 x 19 ¾ (38.1 x 50.1).

156. Rocks, Sea and Sky 1956-57;
14 x 17 7/8 (35.5 x 45.4).

157. Sentinel Rocks 1963; 16 x 19 ¾ (40.7 x 50.2).

158. Rocks and Spray 1961; 28 x 36 (71.1 x 91.4).

159. Stonemason, lithograph;
16 ¼ x 13 ½ (41.2 x 34.3).
Peaches and Mulberry Leaves c.1955;
28 x 36 (71.1 x 91.4).

160. Looking Down from a Height 1955-59;
23 ½ x 29 (59.7 x 73.7).

161. Dancers c.1969; 28 ½ x 21 ½ (72.3 x 54.6).

162. Rocks and Storm 1956-58; 26 x 38 (66 x 96.5).

163. Rocks and Sea, Great Orme, N.Wales c.1963;
12 ¼ x 19 ½ (31.1 x 49.5).

164. Young Ancestor, lithograph;
26 ½ x 15 ½ (67.3 x 39.3).
Shipwreck 1935, pencil; 11 x 9 ½ (28 x 24.1).

165. Wreck of the Early Hope 1960;
36 x 48 (91.4 x 122).

166. A Toute à L'Heure 1961-67, oil, collage;
48 x 60 (122 x 91.4).

167. Armchair Clown, lithograph; 18 ¾ x 13 (47.6 x 33).

168. Icarus 1962-67, casein tempera; 36 x 48 (91.4 x 122).

169. November 22nd 1963; 18 x 23 ¼ (45.7 x 59).

170. Invocation 1965; 16 x 20 (40.7 x 50.8).

171. Of the Company of St Philemon, lithograph;
19 ¼ x 29 ¼ (48.8 x 74.3).

172. Christ on the Sea of Galilee c.1963;
28 x 36 (71.1 x 91.4).

173. Road to Emmaus c.1959; 19 ¾ x 26 (50.2 x 66).
Still Life with Fishes and Bread 1961;
28 x 36 (71.1 x 91.4).

174. Stage Actors, Adam and Eve, lithograph;
22 ½ x 17 ¾ (57.1 x 45.1).
Jacob's Ladder 1966, casein tempera;
16 ¾ x 13 ¼ (42.5 x 33.6).

175. Yellow Rose in Glass c.1966; 20 x 16 (50.8 x 40.7).
Clown with Striped Hat, coloured lithograph;
23 x 17½ (58.4 x 44.4).

176. September Moon 1971-72, acrylic;
25 x 30 (63.5 x 76.2).

177. Christ Mocked, lithograph;
16 ¼ x 11 (41.2 x 27.9).

178. Actor, lithograph; 18 ½ x 15 7/8 (47 x 40.3).

179. Still Life with Pear, Cheese and Cup 1963;
28 x 36 (71.1 x 91.4).

180. Clown with Love Letter, coloured lithograph;
20 ½ x 12 (52.1 x 30.5).

181. Mama's Sunset 1966; 12 x 16 (30.5 x 40.7).

182. Bip as Matador 1975, watercolour;
21 x 17 ½ (53.3 x 44.5).

191. Self Portrait or 'Tales My Mother Told Me'
1959, charcoal; 25 5/8 x 16 ¾ (65 x 42.5).

192. Buziau c.1962; 20 ¼ x 14 ¼ (51.4 x 36.2).
Buziau in Top Hat c.1962;
14 x 11 ¼ (35.5 x 28.5).

193. Young White Face, lithograph;
22 ½ x 17 ¼ (57.1 x 43.8).
Jailed Ancestor c.1969; conté crayon, collage;
25 x 19 (63.5 x 48.2).

194. Harry Langdon, lithograph;
23 x 18 (58.4 x 45.7).
Johannes, coloured lithograph;
28 x 20 ¼ (71.1 x 51.4).

195. Flurry of Snow, November 1970, acrylic;
16 x 20 (40.7 x 50.8).

196. The Leap 1967; 25 x 30 (63.5 x 76.2).

197. Lovers 1969, casein tempera; 20 x 16 (50.8 x 40.7).

198. Fading Ray of Sun 1968, acrylic;
25 x 30 (63.5 x 76.2).

199. The Wave 1968, acrylic; 25 x 30 (63.5 x 76.2).

200. Stepping Out, coloured lithograph;
13 ¾ x 9 ½ (34.9 x 24.1).

201. Oasis 1964-65, casein tempera;
16 x 20 (40.7 x 50.8).

202. Head in the Clouds, lithograph;
22 ¾ x 17 ¼ (57.7 x 43.7).

203. My Brother and I, lithograph (not initialled);
18 x 12 ½ (45.7 x 31.7).

204. Dancer, lithograph;
22 ¼ x 17 ¾ (56.5 x 45.1).

205. Top Hat, lithograph; 17 7/8 x 14 ¼ (45.3 x 36.1).

206. Buster (Keaton), lithograph;
17 ¾ x 16 ½ (45.1 x 41.8).

207. Painter with Notebook 1968,
16 x 20 (40.7 x 50.8).
Daphne, coloured lithograph;
22 ¼ x 17 ½ (56.5 x 44.4).

208. Clown in Black Hat, lithograph;
19 5/8 x 11 5/8 (49.8 x 29.5).

210. The Meeting of Theo and Vincent Van Gogh
in Paradise 1974, acrylic; 48 x 36 (122 x 91.4).

211. White Face, Braided Hat, lithograph;
23 x 17 ¾ (58.4 x 45.1).

212. White Face in Straw Hat, lithograph;
22 x 17 (55.8 x 43.1).

213. Last Will and Testament 1966;
18 x 23 (45.8 x 58.4).

214. Pills Yet More Pills 1961-63; 28 x 18 ¾ (71.1 x 47.6).

215. What is the Time? lithograph;
22 x 17 (55.8 x 43.1).

217. World Upside Down 1966-67;
30 ¾ x 22 ¼ (78.1 x 56.5).

218. Head in a Niche, lithograph;
20 ¼ x 15 ½ (51.4 x 39.3).
Understudy, lithograph; 18 x 14 ½ (45.7 x 36.8).

219. Poet 1967; 28 x 24 (71.1 x 61).

220. Pelléas and Mélisande 1967; 16 x 20 (40.7 x 50.8).

221. Chopin 1960; 28 ¼ x 19 ¾ (71.7 x 50.2).

222. Black Rock 1966; 16 ¼ x 20 ¼ (41.2 x 51.4).

223. Cleft Tree, lithograph; 15 ¼ x 19 7/8 (38.7 x 50.5).

224. Rain 1968, acrylic; 25 x 30 (63.5 x 76.2).

232. Clown Conjurer c.1967, watercolour, collage;
18 ¼ x 12 ½ (46.3 x 31.8).

233. Hope 1968, acrylic; 16 x 20 (40.7 x 50.8).

234. Walk to the Moon, Childhood Command
1967-69; 25 x 30 (63.5 x 76.2).

235. The Fall of Icarus and the Triumph 1971-72,
acrylic; 48 x 36 (122 x 91.5).

236. Elegy to Lost Fishermen 1973, acrylic;
36 x 48 (91.5 x 122).

237. Dreaming Clown 1974-75, acrylic;
60 x 50 (152.5 x 127).

238. Carnival Kings 1974, acrylic;
36 x 48 (91.5 x 122).

239. St Philemon, Painted Horse and Clowns 1973-75,
acrylic; 96 x 57¼ (244 x 145.4).

240. Moon, Muse and Poet Clown 1972-73, acrylic;
30 x 40 (76.2 x 101.8).

241. White Face Clown against Cavernous
Backcloth 1972, acrylic; 30 x 25 (76.2 x 63.5).

242. Bouquet in a Pottery Jar 1973, acrylic;
24 x 20 (61 x 50.8).

243. Smiling Clown 1974, acrylic; 18 x 14 (45.8 x 35.5).

244. Aunt Sally's Sister 1973, acrylic;
14 x 10 (35.5 x 25.4).

245. Clown with Broad-brimmed Hat 1978, acrylic;
12 x 10 (30.5 x 25.4).

246. Walk to the Moon, Childhood Admonishment
1975, acrylic; 92 x 40; (234 x 101.5).

247. Fisherman and Burning Bush 1963-73;
36 x 28 (91.5 x 71).

Addendum

Works belonging to The Albert Houthuesen Trust are credited 'AHT'.

Each work illustrated in *Walk To The Moon* will be reproduced
in the Houthuesen catalogue raisonné being prepared by Richard Nathanson.

The lithographs reproduced were each published in a limited, numbered edition
of 100 prints, stamped with the publisher's mark. Each print is black and white and
initialed in the plate, unless otherwise stated. A representative selection is in Tate Britain.

Richard Nathanson is working on the artist's biography which will include an in-depth
examination of the work. He can be contacted at *richard@richardnathanson.co.uk*;
and would be pleased to hear from those with pictures and letters by the artist –
also photographs and memories of him.

An extract from the 1976 BBC film *Walk To The Moon* on the artist's life,
can be viewed, with other information, on *www.houthuesen.com*.

Published by

The Putney Press
P.O.Box 515, London SW15 2WB, U.K.
Tel: 00 44 (0) 208 788 2718
Email: *info@theputneypress.co.uk*

Printed and bound in Great Britain by Biddles Ltd, Norfolk.

ISBN – 978-0-9516219-2-9